A
GENERAL'S
INSIGHTS
INTO
LEADERSHIP
AND
MANAGEMENT

REORGANIZING

CONSOLIDATING

DOWNSIZING

CHARLES R. HENRY
Major General
U.S. Army (Retired)

A Senior Business General
in the Department of Defense
1988–1992

BATTELLE PRESS
Columbus • Richland

Library of Congress Cataloging-in-Publication Data

Henry, Charles R., 1937–
    A general's insights into leadership and management: reorganizing,
consolidating, downsizing / by Charles R. Henry.
        p.   cm.
    Includes index.
    ISBN 1-57477-000-4. — ISBN 1-57477-013-6 (pbk.)
    1. Leadership. 2. Management.   I. Title.
    HD57.7.H445   1995   95-33082
    658.4'092–dc20   CIP

Cover design by Brown & Associates, Columbus, Ohio
Photo by Kenneth Garrett/FPG International

Battelle Press
505 King Avenue
Columbus, OH 43201–2693
614–424–6393
Toll Free: 1–800–451–3543
Fax: 614–424–3819

ACKNOWLEDGMENTS

I have often remarked that when I pinned on the one star of a brigadier general, it was difficult to get those around me to tell it to me like it is. In fact, I believe that leaders must go out of their way to create an atmosphere that encourages those around them to speak freely and offer their true opinions.

This is not so with one's spouse. Certainly the person one lives with is a person's best critic. I have often broken the ice with an audience by relating that while shaving and contemplating what I was going to tell them, I had mused, "I wonder how many great men there are in the world today?" To which my wife would respond, "One less than you think, bud!" Funny, but so true. My wife, Sandy, is my best advisor. While I may not always acknowledge this fact to her, I do now publicly. She also spent 32 years with me in the United States Army. We were married during my junior year in college, and I was commissioned a second lieutenant two years later, in 1959. The Army moved her 22 times in those 32 years as I was assigned duties around the world. Along the way she raised two very fine children, Kathryn and Mark, of whom I am extremely proud. Mark married a wonderful lady, Leigh Anne Lollar, and they have given Sandy and me our two wonderful granddaughters, Dianna Frances and Virginia Leigh.

This book has been a thought piece for me. Mark, now a lieutenant in the United States Navy, would often ask advice and "guidance" on different aspects of leadership. Naturally, I was only too happy to give my son advice, and I appreciate him asking as often as he did. This series of discussions got me started on discussing leadership and management topics.

Kathryn, a college journalism major, and Leigh Anne, a college English major, took on the job of editing the manuscript drafts by cutting and consolidating the material into a readable text. Sandy transcribed the material from tapes, and produced numerous editions until we felt it ready to go to the publishers; she also gave me invaluable advice on construction. To each of them I owe a great debt of thanks and my personal gratitude for all the hours they individually labored over the manuscript. A lot of dinner conversations were centered around this book.

This book is dedicated to:

Sandy

Kathryn

Leigh Anne

Mark

A special dedication goes to my granddaughters, Dianna and Virginia. May the leaders of their day understand the wisdom of "accomplish the mission, and take care of the employee."

CHARLES R. HENRY
Washington D.C.

FOREWORD

The words "leadership" and "management" are closely related and are often used interchangeably. Nevertheless, in the military, a great distinction is made between them. To oversimplify, management is usually associated with things and leadership relates to people.

A major emphasis of all of our military services is on the development of leadership, in the battle sense, to fight and win wars. However, it also is recognized that high quality management plays a key role in our National Defense Program. Consequently, military officers are trained both to lead in the military sense and to understand and become managers. The United States Department of Defense is the largest institution of its kind in the world. Its annual budget exceeds a quarter of a trillion dollars. It is complex, bureaucratic, and very diverse, reflecting service cultures that, with the exception of the Air Force, are more than 200 years old. Aside from the men and women in uniform, tens of thousands of civilians are employed by the Department of Defense or one of its agencies. This is to say nothing of the vast outreach to the private sector that occurs in contracting for weapon systems, supplies, and a myriad of other essentials necessary to build the fighting force the country needs.

The last 20 years have seen monumental changes in the organization and operation of the Department of Defense. These changes extend well beyond Washington and impact our forces worldwide. Most civilians are not aware of these epic changes.

The All Volunteer Force established in 1973 was tested in Desert Storm when Americans became aware of the high quality of the men and women who serve us in uniform, as well as

their skills across a broad range of endeavors. Success by our
service members in the Persian Gulf, however, relied heavily on
logistics backup. There also has been a dramatic drawdown of
our Armed Forces since the fall of the Berlin Wall in November
of 1989; but before that historic event, powerful forces were at
work in the Department. Both downsizing and a consolidation
of functions has occurred on the procurement side, much of
which can be attributed to the sweeping Goldwater/Nichols Act
that went well beyond the general perception of simply
strengthening the Joint Chiefs of Staff. Reform also was inspired
by implementation of the sweeping recommendations of the
Packard Commission. As a result, Department contracting, including procurement and all phases of acquisition, as well as research and development, embarked on a new way of doing
business. Downsizing the contracting functions started at the
Pentagon in the late 1980s and has gained momentum since.

This book, written by a General Officer who not only was a
leader of the process, but was also an astute observer of what
was occurring, chronicles that change. It discusses the application of principles of leadership to the requirements of management. At the heart of military operations are quality people.
The author takes that principle and relates it to the management side of our Department of Defense. There is a key inter-
relationship between successful military operations and the
effective management of procurement.

General Henry, who was given the enormous challenge of
forming a major new command for contract management for the
entire Department of Defense, discusses how he approached the
challenge from the vantage point of a military leader. Obviously,
as you read the book, it is clear that the General "wore his stars
lightly." Although in charge of a vast command with thousands
of people, and billions of dollars in expenditures, he resisted the
temptation to take himself too seriously.

This book is about basics. It applies common sense to solving complex problems. It has been observed that experience is
what you get when you are looking for something else. General
Henry brought his more than 30 years of military experience to
guiding the change of a vast institution of our government

which, despite the many slings and arrows it has received, is a remarkably effective organization, thanks in part to the author.

This is a book not just about the military, rather it is a book about people and how to get the best from them. Not only the military commander, but the corporate executive can learn from it.

THE HONORABLE JOHN O. MARSH, JR.
Former Secretary of the Army

CONTENTS

PREFACE

A. J. Stinnett has been a long-time friend and advisor to me in my public and professional life. We first met when I directed the Cleveland, Ohio, office of contract administration for the Department of Defense (DoD). Stinnett is a management consultant in Columbus, Ohio, who specializes in the effective management of organizations. His advice, counsel, and friendship to me over the years has been invaluable.

In 1988, when the DoD announced that I had been chosen to lead the Defense Contracts Administration Services, a part of the Defense Logistics Agency, Stinnett said to me, "You are now at the top of your career path (military procurement); you are going to experience some interesting leadership and management challenges. I advise you to record your observations of these challenges."

I took to heart Stinnett's advice, and during the 4½ years that I occupied the office, I made daily notes on happenings about leadership and management and especially my observations of events. These notes, made on 3 x 5-inch cards that I always carried, were often made during the long and boring meetings that are so much a part of life with large organizations.

I did not originally make these notes with any thought of writing this book. Rather, in commanding an organization of 20,000 people, I felt that I needed to record my observations so that I could effectively address these leadership and management issues as the organization moved forward.

Things really got interesting when two senior members of the Bush Administration, Deputy Secretary of Defense Donald Atwood and Under Secretary of Defense for Acquisition John

Betti, sought, and directed the management and leadership of consolidating nearly all Army, Navy, Air Force, and Defense Department procurements that dealt with administering contracts the American defense industry worked on at the contractor's manufacturing facility.

This was no small task. At its peak, the organization would authorize payments to the defense industry at a rate of **$60 million an hour**. I had the good fortune to be selected to break up the old bureaucracy and build a new, more efficient, more effective organization.

With the notes Stinnett encouraged me to make, along came the opportunity to implement what I had learned in creating for DoD its largest business organization, which had worldwide interests. This gives true meaning to the old saying, "It is better to be lucky than good."

In writing this book, I have presumed that these observations have value for the personal and professional lives of others. As a general officer in the United States Army, many younger officers sought my advice. As a result, I have concluded that it really does not matter to which organization a person belongs, be it military or civilian, government or commercial, the basics are the same. The only difference is the intensity with which one operates.

Therefore, I have designed this book to give you, the reader, some real-world advice on how to act or react, how to plan, what to do, and what not to do in organizational settings. The book also addresses how to conduct yourself as you pursue the daily course of business. While I have written from a military perspective, and draw on military experiences, I feel that managers in the business world will be able to adapt the general principles and axioms I propose to that environment.

At the beginning of the book, I describe how we established the Defense Contract Management Command. I am indebted to A. J. Stinnett for his additional management advice as we formed this new and far-reaching organization. I hope readers will find my rumination on the subject interesting. I chose to address my observations concerning the formation of this new command in Part I in the hope that it will establish credibility in the reader's mind about the validity of my advice concerning organizational leadership issues and individual career-development characteristics. As I discuss the basics of organizational leadership through the next three parts of the book, I refer frequently to events and people described in this first part. All this experience and reflection led to the checklist of significant leadership and management observations that concludes the book. Leaders can reflect on these observations, accept them, or reject them at their pleasure.

I make no claims that I am the originator of each and every leadership or management trait discussed in this book. In the course of 32 years of leadership, I have adopted many fundamentals from others. I experimented with them and, if they worked, I adopted them as my own. I think leadership traits are something you must practice until you become comfortable with them. Employing the accumulation of many individual traits will produce a distinctively unique leader. Since effective leadership is the accumulation of good management practices, it is doubtful that anyone can be the total originator of a new wave of leadership functions. Rather, the most successful leaders are those who take the basic leadership points and arrange them in a manner that fits the person's personality as they constantly apply them in their working environment.

The experienced, mature, and successful leader could argue that there is not much new in this book, and I would certainly not disagree with that assertion. But I hope the person still experimenting with leadership can find a trait that can become an "old friend" just as I have. It has been my experience that each time a leader uses certain techniques with success, it builds confidence. Thus, an accumulation of successful traits produces the type of leader that a person becomes.

In the end, if there is a nugget of information that a reader finds informative; and, better yet, if a reader adopts as his or her own a comment that proves to be beneficial, my effort in writing this book is justified.

INTRODUCTION

Creating the
Defense Contract
Management Command

STARTING THE ENGINE

On February 26. 1990, John Betti, the Under Secretary of Defense for Acquisition officially established the Defense Contract Management Command (DCMC) at the Defense Logistics Agency (DLA) in Cameron Station, Virginia. Deputy Secretary of Defense Donald J. Atwood directed that the new DCMC would administer defense contracts where the work is performed—at the contractor's plant—and consolidate nearly all contract administration for the Department of Defense (DoD) worldwide. The DCMC operation would later serve as a model for the Bush administration's Defense Management Review.

As deputy director of the DLA, I was to be responsible for the new command. My acceptance speech took only 5 minutes. I said:

> To the soldiers, sailors, airmen, and marines of the U.S. Armed Forces, we will provide nothing but the best quality goods, on time, and where you need them. To the Army, Navy, Air Force, Marine Corps, and Coast Guard, we will establish a command that will be an extension of your program manager's office. Where you have a problem, we have a problem. Only when you are satisfied, will we be satisfied. To the defense contractor, large and small, we will make doing

business with the defense department as simple and efficient as possible. If you give us a quality product within cost and on time, we will minimize our oversight of your operation. To the employees of the defense department's contract administration community, we will minimize the disruptions in your life as the transition to the new command takes place. We will provide you with a work environment where success is appropriately recognized and adequately rewarded. To the military who serve in these important joint-duty assignments, we will create an environment that benefits fully from your military experience. To our overseas customers and contractors, we will provide the same level of customer support as we do to those closer to the flag pole. To our allies, we will treat you as valued customers. And, to the citizens of this country—the taxpayers who ultimately foot the bill—we will create a new command that is a model of efficiency and effectiveness.

A short speech, but a strong commitment. Larry Wilson, public affairs officer of DLA, and I had worked on the format, and this simple speech was our commitment to the future.

After the speech, Betti was ecstatic. He told me he felt that was the kind of commitment that we needed in government, and he asked that I put the speech on a poster and send him a copy to hang in his office. Buoyed by his comment, we made the posters and distributed them throughout the command . . . and the world.

The simple principles in the speech set us on a course to ensure that we fulfilled each one. The final result was my report to the Secretary of Defense, delivered on November 24, 1992, which stated:

As I leave the Defense Logistics Agency after nearly three years as the first commander of the Defense Contract Management Command, it is my privilege to provide you with an assessment of consolidated DoD contract management. I am pleased to report that by *the end of 1993, the command will have reduced or avoided $525 million in the cost of performing contract administration since its establishment in February 1990. In fact, we exceeded our original goal of reducing 2,155 people by the second quarter of fiscal year 1991, and we saved $255 million by the second quarter of fiscal year 1992. The other cost reductions were the result of workload reduction, streamlining, and more effective business practices. Further, DCMC transferred 44 service plant representative offices (subordinate organizations), some 5,400 personnel, and 100,000 contracts worth $400 billion from the military department in June of 1990. We then closed five intermediate headquarters around the country and found jobs for virtually all displaced workers; only 15 persons were involuntarily terminated. By October 1990, we had transferred a large portion of the overseas contract administration workload and created an overseas operation.*

DCMC continues to pursue the cornerstone of its operational concept of having the right people, in the right number, at the right places, at the right time, doing the right things. We identified our strategy to support this concept with four elements: empowering employees, teaming to achieve a seamless approach to problem solving, identifying and meeting customer requirements, and continuously improving the work process. This we accomplished by providing more value for the American taxpayer.

Along the way, as a student of leadership and management, I made certain observations about what works in large and detailed organizations. What follows is an observation about leadership and management from the unique perspective I gained by commanding this highly successful organization: attributes that I think can be applied in any organization, business as well as military. I hope that the reader finds the observations as important and interesting as I have found them upon reflection.

ADMINISTERING CONTRACTS

Very briefly, my report to the Secretary of Defense stated what DCMC accomplished in pursuing its strong commitment. But, where were the roots of this organization? In the early 1960s, a program known as Project 60 sought to consolidate the military departments under one contract administration. The fundamental principle was that a procuring contracting officer located in the military departments would award a contract. Subsequently, if contract administration was to be performed at a contractor facility, the procuring contracting officer would delegate the contract to an "administrative contracting officer," who would be part of the Defense Contracts Administration Services (DCAS).

In 1964, after this initial consolidation (resulting in the creation of the DCAS), the military departments said, "Now, we don't mind giving up this kind of operation for most of the small, insignificant contracts—those contracts that do not have a lot of visibility (nor a lot of interest or intensity)—but where we have the "crown jewels" (the B-1 aircraft bombers, the Army Apache helicopters, the B-2 airplanes for example), we would like to retain the contract administration services and perform the entire procurement function from `cradle to grave.'"

Initially, that makes a very logical argument; and, at the time, DoD accepted it and granted the exceptions. However, by 1990 the exceptions had grown enormously; in fact, the total cost of contracts excepted totaled the net worth of contracts administered by DCAS—approximately $400 billion! The Air Force had excepted $200 billion worth of contracts with 26 different locations and had placed a two-star general in charge of the operation. The Navy had 13 locations where they also excepted about $200 billion, and that did not include ship building. (Ship building is still excluded at this writing from the concept of consolidation of contract administration.) The end result was that DoD had almost $400 billion worth of business under the DCAS, the organization originally formed to consolidate and streamline the contract management, and an additional $400 billion in business between the Air Force and the Navy that had been excepted! The Army had a mere five plants excepted and was the biggest supporter of DCAS in the beginning—most likely because they did not look at contract administration as a major threat. Then too, the Army was a big contributor of personnel and leadership to DCAS. The Army appeared to be perfectly willing for others to administer and accept the quality of their products.

Contract administration actually involves several functions. Administrative Contracting Officers (ACO) have a warrant allowing them to represent the government; quality assurance specialists are in the contractor's plant, pass on the contractor's assembly line procedures, and finally accept the product; and production specialists assist the ACOs in determining if the contractor is on cost and schedule. These professionals must administer the contract and interface with the contractor, make any change in orders, negotiate for future rate increases, and complete final negotiations. Large contracting is a continuous process, and it needs competent professionals to constantly work with the contractor. Finally and hopefully, the government can accept a quality product. The end result is that someone from the United States government must accept the product (as conforming to specifications). The government representative must then sign DoD Form 250 authorizing the contractor to receive payment from the finance officer. Additionally under DCMC, the Directorate of Program and Technical Support, under the leadership of a flag officer (admiral or general) would supervise a strong interface between the program management offices of the military and contract administrators in the plants. In Washington, the primary purpose was to associate with the program managers to ensure that, from their viewpoint, the contract administration personnel were giving their professional advice and assistance. We found that in the past, the program managers did not know what they expected of contract administration. The services were perfectly willing to award the contract, send it down to the contractor to perform, and wait patiently for the item to come out on the other end of the contractor's production line. Truth of the matter is, it almost never, if ever, happens that way.

PROVIDING BEST VALUE

In October of 1988, as the problems in contract administration mounted, Under Secretary of Defense Robert Costello called me at DLA and asked if I would put together a group of acquisition professionals and report back to him on how best to provide incentive for the American defense industry to improve product quality and minimize costs. I called Rear Admiral Robert Moore, now Chief, U.S. Navy Supply Corps; Anthony DeLuca, who was the Air Force Competition Advocate General at the time; Major General Harry Karegeannes, Chief of Army procurement; and Brigadier General William Fedorochko, who was a member of Costello's staff.

We met frequently over a two-month period. Each of us had extensive experience in buying goods and services for DoD; each of us had been asked to perform duties in the acquisition arena that were different from the norm; and each of us had in his past been called upon to exercise unique judgment to determine a new and innovative method to do the job. We worked very hard to answer Costello's question, and we produced some recommendations that we felt had merit. I have found that Washington has no shortage of smart people who can make good recommendations on tough issues. The key is to get an action plan that the leadership will follow in implementing the recommendations.

We did not give Costello an implementing plan, but we gave him a series of recommendations that we felt, if implemented, would produce what we were to term "best value." While no one will probably remember the specifics of the recommendations today, the term "best value" survived and was even picked up in legislative language later. In 1995, when one talks about good acquisition practices, the term "best value" generally is used. "Best value," reduced to its simplest terms, means "All factors being equal, the technical factors considered and evaluated first, price becomes the determinate factor."

This changes the concept of most people that government contracts always go to the low bidder. The acquisition community must first determine what it wants, then industry must respond by offering an item that meets the technical specifications of the requirement. Only when this is done does price become an issue; and, in this case, the lowest responsive bidder should be the one who receives the award. Would-be contractors who cannot offer an item that meets the requirement should not be given an award simply because they bid lower than a responsible bidder. This concept, implemented throughout the acquisition community, provided "best value" for the American taxpayer as well as for the military service person.

ESTABLISHING THE COMMAND

After President George Bush assumed office, Donald Atwood was nominated for the position of deputy secretary of defense. Shortly thereafter and before his confirmation, I received a call from David Berteau, a senior DoD official whom I knew and highly respected (he later became the deputy assistant secretary of defense for production and logistics). He asked me to come talk to Atwood about the contract administration for DoD. (At the time I was the head of DCAS, the predominate arm of the department for operating contract administration.) Those of us working in contract administration knew that a consolidation would be in the best interest of the American taxpayer, but we also knew that it would take a heavy hand to make any real change. We quickly discovered two things: One, it's simple and easy to determine what needs to be done. But, two, there is another whole body of work in determining how to do it.

Prior to the Atwood meeting, Berteau alerted me that we should start thinking about how we could consolidate contract management into a separate agency. I had a plan in mind. So when Berteau called to say Atwood wanted a meeting, I was ready. We talked about an hour and a half on the subject. At the conclusion of our meeting, Atwood looked at me and said, "I'm ready to authorize this. I just need to be confirmed by the Senate." I left the meeting knowing that finally a major event in the consolidation of defense contract administration was about to take place. It was only a question of when.

In early 1990, more than 26,000 people were employed in contract management from all services. The total dollar value of the contracts under supervision was approximately $780 billion. In February 1989, President Bush, speaking to a joint session of Congress, directed the Secretary of Defense to develop a plan to improve the defense procurement process and management at the Pentagon. Previously, former Deputy Secretary of Defense David Packard had chaired a commission that concluded that consolidating and streamlining DoD's contract administration function would improve its management effectiveness. This opinion led directly to establishment of the Defense Contract Management Task Force in April 1989, under the leadership of my immediate supervisor, General Charles McCausland. Under Secretary Betti envisioned a single agency supervising all contract administration for all of the military services. This umbrella included those contracts presently administered by DLA and added those administered by the military departments—Army, Navy, and Air Force. This new agency would ideally report to the under secretary (for acquisition) and be charged with more effectively performing the contract administration mission.

Betti approved the plan to establish a single contract management organization on October 1, 1989. The plan would not only streamline existing contract administration organizations, but would promote uniform procurement policies, update the quality of the contract administration work force, and eliminate overhead by reducing payroll costs. The plan would also make appropriate provisions for continued technical and other support to program offices of the services. In addition, the plan would preserve the existing regulatory divisions of responsibility between the administrative contracting officer of DCMC and the procuring contracting officers, which would continue to be the responsibility of the military departments.

When McCausland took control of the Defense Contract Management Task Force, he assigned me the fundamental task of running the day-to-day operation. At the time, I was deputy director of DLA for acquisition management, overseeing more than $12 billion worth of procurement a year and buying all the food, fuel, medical supplies, clothing, and some spare parts for

DoD. The other part of my job—a substantial part—was administering DCAS.

The old DCAS and the various service-owned contract administration organizations, with their bureaucracies, formed a real "hodgepodge" structure. In effect, the system had four sets of rules, procedures, and forms—all prescribing business in different ways. A contractor who was working for the Army, Navy, Air Force, and DoD through DLA would literally have to follow four different sets of procedures—resulting in a tremendous cost for both the government and the contractor. Consider that in 1989, the average government employee working in a contractor's plant earned approximately $40,000 a year. We can reasonably assume that the average cost for the defense contractor to place a person in the plant to respond to the government representative should equal that of a government employee. Consequently, the American taxpayer paid $80,000 for the interface between the two.

There are other problems as well. On two occasions over the past 15 years, I performed a sample survey that indicated up to 38 percent of all contracts go delinquent at some point in their life. In the early 1990s, with 1,200 defense contractors reporting, more than 440,000 material deficiencies (individual incidents that indicated the contractor did not produce an item that met the required quality standard) were requested. While not necessarily "junk," these items do not, for whatever reason, meet the quality standard. A Material Review Board is convened to decide on the disposition of these items. To determine a course of action, the Board reviews the contract, the specifications, and what the contractor produced.

In most cases, the product is too good to scrap, but, nevertheless, does not meet specifications. The government representative cannot legally accept the item. The options may be that the government would accept the item at a reduced price or reject it entirely. In this case, the contractor must rework the item.

The significance is that, of 440,000 Material Review Board actions, between 17 and 21 million individual pieces were offered to the Government that did not meet contract requirements (1991). This meant that at least 15 to 20 percent of the item cost was in some form of inefficiency. If the government and industry could reduce that inefficiency, several benefits would accrue. The American taxpayers would benefit. The soldier, sailor, airman, and marine would get a better product because it would be what was asked for in the beginning. Contractors would make more money because they would simply reduce the inefficiency by eliminating scrap, rework, and other nonconformities in the manufacturing process. This would be a win-win situation.

From this point of view, and armed with this information, we set about to change the process and increase the quality of items produced for the defense industry.

At this point we asked fundamental questions: What do we do well? What do we do poorly? What should we change? What should we leave alone? What could be the future if we build an organization that would be responsive to both the Department of Defense and the taxpayer?

Each branch of the service gave us the help of their top professionals to answer these questions as well as, "What, in their opinion, would the best contract management organization look like?" These people were true professionals and genuinely concerned with improving a process that, in effect, consumed one and a half billion taxpayer dollars a year. We proceeded on the premise that, if a process could reduce the cost of defense acquisition, we would be better able to serve the American taxpayer. These professionals devoted about 17,000 collective hours answering the questions. They had no axe to grind, and we heard little of parochial comments as to whether or not implementation would be good for the Navy, Army, Air Force, etc. They answered the questions succinctly, and their combined effort blended well.

In the fall of 1989, the task force reported its results to McCausland and presented him an execution plan, which he then presented to Betti. The report prescribed the formation of the Defense Contract Management Agency. The agency would be headed by a flag officer at the three-star level and would report directly to the under secretary of defense for acquisition. At that September meeting, when McCausland, Betti, and I were discussing forming a new agency, Betti asked McCausland, "Is it possible for you to establish this as a command under DLA and make it work?"

Naturally, any military individual worth his or her salt is going to respond affirmatively to such a question. McCausland replied, "Yes. We can do it." The truth of the matter was that McCausland's leadership and his relationship with his two deputies was such that he operated the command very much like a chairman of the board of a major corporation. He directed that his two deputies, Rear Admiral Brady Cole, United States Navy, and I, function as corporate presidents of various subsidiaries. Betti appeared to be hesitant about making the bold sweep of creating a new agency with a new overhead structure. He had confidence in the efficiency of DLA and directed McCausland to form the Defense Contract Management Command. A command, not an agency. The command would be a major subordinate element of DLA.

As we left the Pentagon and drove the 4 miles to DLA headquarters at Cameron Station, McCausland looked at me and said, "Chuck, you've got it. I want you to form the command. We'll make it an additional duty to your role as deputy director. Take charge and move out." I responded, "Yes, sir." I knew then that the chance to receive a third star had eluded me. The job graded out in personnel terms as a lieutenant general, but putting it under the existing agency would make it difficult, if not impossible to try to promote the individual heading the command. However, while promotion is always good for the ego, I was looking forward to serving and building this contract administration organization. I had advanced professionally in the procurement function of the army and had held just about every command job in contract administration. I was at the top of my professional discipline, and I was working for one of the greatest logistical generals our country had developed. It was a pleasure to go to work. I set about to make the new command work with all the zeal I could muster. When I returned to headquarters, I called Robert (Bob) Scott, my special assistant, into my office. "Bob, we've got the green light to form the organization, not as an agency, but as a command. Let's make this the best organization we can," I said.

Thus began the most exciting time of creating and operating a large business organization with more than a billion dollar annual budget. The organization would later boast that it authorized payment to defense contractors at a rate of $60 million a work hour.

BUILDING THE COMMAND

As expected, the military services were not happy to relinquish a layer of power. Throughout the proceedings and meetings with Betti, they made their play to either defeat the proposal or water it down so that the services would retain some measure of capability to do their own contract administration. However, for the plan to be successful, nearly all contract administration would have to be transferred from each service to the new DCMC. Contracting officers of each service would have to delegate the 83 separate functions of contract administration to an ACO within DCMC.

I recall one stormy meeting with Betti in which Under Secretary of the Navy Dan Howard was taking exception to transferring the Navy's functions to DCMC. He accused the old DCAS of being ineffective and irresponsible. Betti and his aides dismissed the allegation as political rhetoric and continued to support McCausland on forming the command.

The Air Force played a subtler role, indicating it would support the Bush administration on this issue. What the Air Force wanted, however, was a transfer of DCAS, along with the 13 Navy plants, to the Air Force management division in Albuquerque, New Mexico. The Air Force would then become the executive agent for contract administration—in total control.

Betti and Atwood, fully aware of the politics of the issue, remained firm throughout the proceedings. Since DoD was created in 1947, there had been many attempts by the various service secretaries to marshall power. The truth was that until the passage of the Nichols/Goldwater legislation, the military services had paid lip service only to the issue of DoD consolidation.

In practice, each service operated independently. The Air Force, in particular, was very successful in advancing its own agenda. Congress would appropriate money, and the Air Force would continue its programs. The Navy, to a degree, was successful in operating independently, having a large contingent on Capitol Hill who supported naval power. Each of the services had congressional liaison offices on the Hill. It was and is a fundamental service lobbyist effort, and they do it very well. They take their young, brightest, most personable people and assign them to these liaison offices, and these individuals get to know members of Congress and staffers on a routine basis. In 1985, each service, rather than functioning under one large body (DoD), felt it was the one to go straight to Congress and obtain budgetary support. The climate was right for consolidation of contract administration. In June 1990, the services completed the memoranda of agreement that transferred 44 service plant representative offices, 5,500 personnel, more than 100,000 contracts worth more than $400 billion to DCMC. In July, DCMC had 23,783 personnel assigned to it.

We were now in a position to know what the new organization should look like. We knew that we wanted our headquarters located in Cameron Station, Virginia; and we knew that we must have subordinate organizations in the field. We commissioned an advisory group of former DLA directors and others of stature in the field of military procurement to help in our deliberations.

These individuals had no bias concerning the formation of this new command. The issue became how many subordinate organizations the command would ultimately have. We knew we wanted to take out as many intermediate layers of supervision as possible. We also wanted to streamline and knew that would require something different to effect fundamental change in the acquisition process. The options were three, five, or nine regions. We concluded that five would probably provide the span of control that an efficient organization needs. The advisors agreed with us.

Once we decided on five commands, the next question was where they would be located. This was probably one of the most difficult decisions we had to face. In making this decision, we were affecting the very lives and working status of many people. Each of our nine previous districts (regions) had functioned well under the old system. Their boundaries were well established, and they had operated for more than 25 years. Disestablishing a region would mean abolishing 300 to 700 jobs. The first question we faced was where to locate the new headquarters regionally. I assigned the task to Ron Crandell, Regina Bacon, and Colonel Dan Bartlett. They were to assess the environmental impact of closing each one of the regions and reestablishing the new organization in the same or different location. In my mind, we were closing all nine regions and establishing five new districts located in other parts of the country.

The recommendation was as follows: the best places to establish the command were Atlanta, Philadelphia, Boston, Chicago, and Los Angeles. It would mean disestablishing New York, St. Louis, Dallas, and Cleveland. I had been the commander in Detroit in 1981 when it was a subelement of the Cleveland region. I had also been the senior officer in Cleveland from 1982 to 1984. I respected the people in the Cleveland region and admired the great midwestern work ethic. The night before we made the announcement, I admit I had severe reservations. Cleveland, in my opinion, was an excellent operation. I knew the people and felt the infrastructure was better than some of the others we were going to keep open. The same could be said for Dallas. Dallas had long been considered one of the more economically and best run organizations.

So, here I was, faced with a decision to close two of our very best and most progressive offices. As I wrestled with the question the evening before the announcement, Dan Bartlett said, "Don't try to game this. You've been correct up to now. Make the decision on the best evidence, not on emotions." I knew he was right. I did have an emotional attachment to Cleveland; but, if I made a decision that was not based on unbiased logic, then the whole reorganization would be in great jeopardy. I agreed with the plan. The next day we announced to Betti our intentions to close the specific offices. He gave his approval.

DEALING WITH POLITICS

The acquisition command was the first Defense Management Review the Bush Administration attempted. (President Bush had directed Secretary of Defense Dick Cheney to institute a series of management improvements called Defense Management Reviews.) The attitude in Congress was, and still is to some degree, that nobody takes anybody off the government employment rolls in my district, regardless of the reason. To work the issue, we brought in each of the commanders and gave them the plan. I asked the officers, particularly those losing large numbers of personnel or those losing organizations entirely, to contact their congressional representatives, explain what we were doing, and assure them that it would be our intent to offer each person a job.

Probably one of the most fortuitous decisions I made that July set the tone for the entire future. I credit this decision as a major turning point and the one that would guarantee our later success.

At this point, people had been told which operations were to be closed and which were to be reestablished. The stress level was very high. Secretary Atwood said we had 18 months to accomplish the reorganization. The staff gave me a plan that said, " If we have to close nine, establish five, and we have 18 months to do it, then every three plus months, we should disestablish and establish one."

I had just seen Congresswoman Mary Rose Oakar (D-Ohio). While she accepted what the Bush Administration wanted to do, she was not happy. I knew the political issue was tenuous at best because she was capable of throwing a monkey wrench into this whole thing and stopping the effort entirely! I also knew that the employee union in St. Louis was not happy. I had visited the union president and talked with him about why we were closing the St. Louis operation. We had a good relationship. We respected each other; however, I knew that the union was not happy with the idea of closing the St. Louis office. If either Oakar or the union found a "weak link" in our plan, they would crush it. I could not take this chance.

So, at the meeting where my staff was recommending closing and reestablishing a command every three months, it occurred to me that a bold sweep was needed. I asked, "Why don't we just close them all in August (1990), and reestablish five districts at the same time?" You could have heard a pin drop. The staff had not contemplated such a move. I thought we could do it. I turned to my aides and said, "Get me a plane ticket to each location. Tell them I will personally participate in the closing and reestablishing. And give me a plan to do it all in the month of August." With that, I rose and left the room. The staff was wondering how in the world we would accomplish all this in such a short period of time.

In the end, we accomplished it with a sweeping success. Each of the commanders was given a date that was convenient, and I was on travel the entire month of August. However, when we were finished, we had a permanent organization in place in five distinct locations around the country, and not a single word from Congress or the unions. Talk about dumb luck! Those organizations that had been disestablished would now be integrated into the newly established districts.

MANAGING PERSONNEL

We now knew what the new organization would look like. We knew where we wanted our headquarters, and we knew that we must have subordinate organizations in the field. The total number of commands would be five, with around 350 people each. We knew we had more people at each site than we needed in the new organization. The cornerstone of the new organization was to have the right number of people, at the right place, at the right time, doing the right thing. That sounds good, and it is easy to say, but making it happen was no small feat.

In our strategy to support this concept, we identified four essential elements.

First, was empowering employees. Intuitively over the years I've found that if you add layers and layers of management, people at the bottom who are really supposed to do the work do not do the things they should because they feel somebody else is going to check and correct their work. We started slowly, but found that as we empowered people, they took on a greater degree of energy and responsibility about what they were doing.

Second, was getting everyone to "buy in" to the process. When they do, once a decision is made, it becomes easier to implement.

Third, was identifying and meeting customer requirements. This, of course, sounds very academic; however, the concept of a government agency having customers, both internal and external, was relatively new. Although, today it has taken on more importance and seems commonplace, in 1990 it was a new idea.

Fourth, was improving the work process. The system needed a function that could tie into the program manager and provide substantive help. The staff developed a concept that eventually brought great results—the Transition Management Office (TMO). The TMO recognized two organizations at the same site: the permanent new organization and a temporary one that would soon close. In August 1990, when we directed the new organization to begin operating, we did not give out termination notices or reduction-in-force (RIF) notices. But we did try to create a sense of urgency. We stressed that the new organization was going to be the functional organization, and we assigned personnel to permanent jobs in that organization (in accordance with department personnel practices). These people knew their jobs were permanent.

Those people who were not placed within the new organization were transferred to the TMO. I personally told each that he or she was a good employee, valuable to the organization, and that we were going to offer jobs based upon the positions available. I must note that in reorganizations, most government agencies simply hand out "pink slips" and suffer a reduction-in-force. My job was to streamline and organize. My directive from Atwood did not mention that I was to save money or reduce the budget. (Although that is a normal consequence of reorganizations.) I was in control of the money, and I had the luxury of offering everybody a job.

As an aside, this approach offers a lesson for those who wish to reorganize. Find the person to do the task. Delegate the authority to run the show, requiring only a report of bottom line results to the leadership. When the senior financial official, normally the comptroller, starts making business policy or pulls the money from the target organization, those who have to manage are not free to make the best business decision—a disaster in the making.

I made a commitment to all employees that we were going to work very hard to keep them gainfully employed, but I wanted each one to know these jobs were not permanent, that this arrangement was temporary until we could find permanent positions. We would later offer each person at least one or two positions. I even agreed to pay personnel relocation costs. Our estimates indicated it would be cheaper to place these people, some having to take downgrades in rank, than it would be for us to terminate and pay severance. Concurrently, we directed all of our supervisors to hire from inside, not outside, to fill a job.

This attention to the individual had a significant effect upon the organization and our ability to make it a success. We offered everybody in the organization employment. I personally told each employee that if he or she wanted to stay, we would offer a job. Larry Wilson, of public affairs, convinced me to become very visible to the organization by informing them of current events. Wilson developed the *Bugle,* a newsletter to all employees that told them without a lot of fanfare exactly what was happening. (Later, the feedback from the employees indicated that this expression from management about taking care of the people and our commitment to them was comforting since they were able to make decisions about their future.)

While I promised the offer of jobs, I could not guarantee everyone a job at his or her present grade; and in all probability I could not guarantee a job at the same location. But, if they wanted to continue working in contract management, we would find a position for which they were qualified. Al Ressler, the agency's personnel chief, was instrumental in making this work. Ressler had recently joined DLA from the Army's personnel department. He was dynamic and able to make things happen. Ressler said that within DLA (50,000 employees) 20 people either die, resign, or otherwise terminate employment each day. Given the choice to move, retire if eligible, or resign if not, employees would make their own best career decisions. If we controlled (stopped) outside hiring, we could solve our problem. By not hiring new people from the outside and encouraging those who worked for us to take a transfer to where we had jobs, we would be able to complete the organization. That is exactly what happened.

Not surprisingly, however, there was a time lag in filling jobs in the organization. Naturally, our supervisors wanted instant results. If we didn't control the process entirely, they would be inclined to employ a local person. In effect, we would be bringing people into the organization, and kicking people out at the same time. Not a good way to deal with people. My job was to move about 4,000 people around the country/world into different jobs. It took a lot of nurturing, but keeping a total freeze on outside hiring and ensuring that only people displaced within the organization could be hired paid handsomely in the end. Four thousand people went off the employment rolls, but we involuntarily terminated only 15 people. The rest resigned or retired. The decision was theirs. I consider that one of our major accomplishments. Our concern for people's security reaped dividends in employee morale and productivity.

COMMANDING THE DISTRICTS

The initial plan called for a three-star general/admiral as the director, a senior civilian deputy, and one-star general/admiral in the field commanding each of the districts. In my opinion, these were vice-presidents on the operating level. We had also asked for a program and technical executive director at the headquarters. This individual would be either a senior civilian or a general/admiral. My argument was that a billion-dollar-a-year business should have senior leadership in the field. We were administering $750 billion in defense contracts.

Much to my surprise, this argument did not wash with Atwood and Betti. Betti agreed with the importance; but when I asked for approval, he told me to use what I had and work future requests on an individual basis. (I did have two generals out of five already assigned; although the command would subsequently lose authority for these generals, and I would never be able to get others assigned.)

The one exception was Program and Technical Support. Atwood authorized creating a Program and Technical Support directorate, and the Navy gave us Rear Admiral Donald "Smoke" Hickman as the first director. Hickman was a brand new rear admiral, intelligent and very personable.

The services were unsure of us, but they did transfer 800 people who had been performing technical services to the new command. Not all the services, I might add. However, most did transfer contract administration people, and Hickman performed admirably and in a most credible manner. My guidance to Hickman was, "I want you to love the program manager (PM) to death, and when the PM thinks that you work for him and I only pay you, then we've just about got it right." Hickman took on the job with a vengeance and was very successful in establishing this new directorate. He accomplished the mission, and he accomplished it well.

When we added Program and Technical Support as a directorate to the new command, the remains of the old DCAS organization still haunted us. Imagine adding a new chair to the table at the staff meeting, and having to remove someone of lessor rank who had been there. This was the first problem. To staff the new directorate, I decided to take the engineers from the contract management directorate. Over the years, DCAS had seen many power struggles, and removing the engineers from this contracts organization was akin to returning land to the Arabs that the Israelis had claimed in the 1967 war. I had to personally direct the transfer and ensure that the other directorates did not unduly hamper the new organization's mission. It was a constant, though often subtle, effort that lasted until I left the organization.

There were personnel conflicts in the new command. The engineers wanted a separate engineering directorate. I said no.

A large group wanted the senior civilian deputy to be an engineer. I said no to that also because the deputy would need an engineering degree. Then, anyone who wanted to climb to the top would have to be an engineer. Those that were not engineers could not aspire to senior leadership.

Thus, we deliberately structured the number-two position as a general manager without a technical degree. This person could be an engineer or not. This was a significant point because the engineers were seeking the opportunity to predominate. While I respect the engineering community, I was trying to focus the issue on support to the service, PM, and that support was broader than engineering alone.

In the end we were successful. The organization matured and became very competent. The service PMs grew to accept this support function; and, as they accepted program and technical support from DCMC, they had more tolerance for the other contract management functions we provided. Some have said the success of this technical support function was the underpinning of our whole successful reorganization.

The Air Force then disestablished its Contract Management Division at Albuquerque, New Mexico. I felt that the commander of that operation, Brigadier General Kenneth Miller, would be just the officer to head up DCMC's western operation in Los Angeles, California. Miller was a particularly good choice; it showed how we could truly integrate the organizations. We accomplished two things with this assignment. First, we kept an Air Force officer involved in very sensitive Air Force contracts, for example, the B-1 and C-17 aircraft. Second, we kept the same officer involved in reorganizing personnel for closing the old Air Force operation. In the end, the Air Force was more receptive because of this assignment.

Miller was enthusiastic, hard working, and very successful. I developed tremendous respect for the Air Force and the way it disestablished its old Contract Management Division. I particularly respected the way the Air Force took care of its people. The Air Force found jobs for all who were displaced and then closed out activities at Albuquerque. We then transferred the remaining operation and the locations from the old DCAS to Los Angeles.

In October 1990, the Air Force had transferred a large portion of the overseas contract administration workload to DCMC. Called the Contract Management Command (CMC) and headquartered at Wright Patterson Air Force Base in Ohio, this unit was predominately concerned with overseas contract management. General Charles McDonald, Commander, Air Force Logistic Command, agreed with DLA's General McCausland to transfer the Air Force CMC operation to DLA "lock, stock, and barrel." He directed that the transfer be accomplished as soon as possible. It was a smooth transfer, without most of the infighting that had accompanied other service organization transfers. McDonald said, "Do it;" and it was done. This was a big relief to me.

We made this unit the center of our foreign operation. My first task was to place Navy Captain Lenn Vincent in charge as its commander. This was a deliberate action. We wanted to establish clearly at the outset that this was a change to joint service activity and also demonstrate that it was a major operational change, not just an organizational change in name only.

Vincent had performed admirably for us on the west coast as the commander of the DCAS Los Angeles district. He impressed me as an individual who would take tough jobs, lead, and inspire the people to follow him. This new international organization was going to be very important and very difficult to manage. We had people very far from headquarters, in fact, all over the world. They were performing different tasks in different ways and dealing with different foreign cultures and, in most cases, different American ambassadors. Vincent's job would be to consolidate these diverse organizations under one command with one set of procedures and rules. He was ready for the task and benefitted from the professional quality of people he inherited from the Air Force.

In addition to Vincent, I assigned John Rayford as the deputy commander. I had worked with Rayford for many years and knew him to be competent. He was well versed in contract administration. He also was exceptionally loyal. I was confident a strong management team was in place.

My confidence was not misplaced. The new international organization took to managing contracts worldwide in a manner that our government had never before been able to do. Soon, I had officers in charge of locations in eight countries with about $15 billion worth of effort. I was very pleased with their success and felt that they were truly giving the American taxpayer value. Vincent was soon ordered to Washington, D.C. and promoted to rear admiral. Later, he became my first choice to replace me when I chose to retire.

With Vincent's promotion, I needed a replacement. I knew I could not put just anyone into this important job, and I liked the idea of putting a naval officer in the middle of Air Force's Wright Patterson Air Force Base—a major base to the Air Force. Thus, I went back to the Navy to get a replacement officer. After looking at many officers, I chose Captain Barry Cohen. Cohen was cut from the same mold as Vincent—savvy, smart, and able to deal with high ranking military officers and civilians, including reluctant U.S. ambassadors. Cohen took over from Vincent and led the organization to greater achievements. What a joy to observe these two fine officers build and lead a worldwide operation.

HEARING BAD NEWS

There's an old adage, "Bad news does not improve with age." In organizations, however, bad news tends to start at the bottom and ages significantly on the way up. People hope they can work the issue and improve it; but the end result is that, as time goes by, the senior manager often is not informed. In defense acquisition, it often takes 30 days before a program manager finds out about a problem from the staff.

DCMC had an organization and group of people who were working in the contractor plant observing contractor performance. Because adverse information was slow in reaching the attention of DoD leadership, Betti, in exasperation, asked for a quicker response program, one that would inform him of problems sooner. We set up such a program and called it the "bell ringer."

A "bell ringer" was anything that would draw significant attention to the program and that DoD senior leaders should know. After we started the program, "bell ringers" came to me with the speed of light. I would decide whether to send the information forward to Betti. In the beginning, those in the field sent everything up, including many insignificant things. As one would expect, program managers were very sensitive about select information going to the top acquisition manager. I personally told each program manager I would not send anything to DoD that the program manager was not personally aware of before hand. Also, if the problem was immediately workable and not something that was going to hit the newspapers the next day, I was perfectly willing to allow the program manager to correct it first or to take it to Betti himself.

"Bell ringers" became a big issue. For the first time in defense acquisition history, the Secretary of Defense's office had a key decision role in what was happening in the defense weapon programs. The service chiefs and the services' assistant secretaries of research, development, and acquisition in effect were losing some of their decision authority over acquisition issues. This came about not from establishing DCMC, but from the Nichols/Goldwater legislation that created the position of under secretary of defense for acquisition. It took a few years after enactment of the legislation for the under secretary's position to mature so that the incumbent was indeed recognized as the senior acquisition official within DoD. Prior to this under secretary role, the services had the absolute final word on acquisition matters. Nichols/Goldwater consolidated operations and put the Secretary of Defense in charge of acquisition. The services did not like this idea and fought it vigorously. Some people in the services were very adept in sheltering information that should have been sent to the Secretary of Defense. No one wanted to have information that was not favorable go outside the organization.

As an example, the Air Force, under a joint agreement with the Navy, was to support the Navy's development of the advance fighter plane and work out of the Air Force plant in Fort Worth, Texas. When the program got in trouble, each service kept any adverse information to themselves. Information that should have gone to the under secretary of defense (acquisition) did not go to him; or, if it did, it was so late that an effective decision could not be made. Because of all the problems, Secretary of Defense Cheney ultimately canceled the Navy's A-12 fighter plane.

Another case in point involved the C-17 transport program produced by McDonnell Douglas Corporation in California. The project was plagued by long delays and cost overruns on a fixed price contract. When a wing collapsed during a test, it was difficult for the Air Force to quickly send the information up the channel to the under secretary of defense. If the "bell ringers" program had not been in place, I question how long it would have been for the word to get from the contractor's plant to the secretary's office. Under the "bell ringer" procedure, as it turned out, the under secretary knew about it within hours. Thus, the Nichols/Goldwater Act was fully implemented and, in my opinion, in the best interest of defense acquisition.

In another case, Betti received a request from a House committee hearing to investigate defense acquisition to talk about the production of the Navy's A-12 advance aircraft. The development of the A-12 was a joint Air Force-Navy effort, with the Navy having a predominate role. DCMC had only recently taken over contract administration of the program. Since DCMC worked for Betti, information on current happenings in the plant were flowing to Betti through normal channels. Although the A-12 administration had just been transferred to DCMC, the people assigned to the A-12 program and in the contractor's plant were summoned to Betti's office and directed to supply him with pertinent factual knowledge. Betti made a decision not to get involved with the details—but to go to the committee and say, "I'm the senior guy. I'm here. The problems did not happen during my employment, but I'm going to clean them up. Just give me time to do it."

This proved to be an ill-fated decision. Betti found himself trying to answer questions about events that happened long before he took the job. He was expected to explain and defend policy matters he could not possibly have known about or have been a party to in the past.

The lesson learned is that when testifying before Congress, bring subject-matter experts with you. Congress allows expert testimony and generally will inquire at the outset about your desire to have an expert testify. Always assume that failure to be totally prepared will result in serious embarrassment. It is not substance but form that necessarily carries the day. Those who highly develop their interpersonal skills and confidence appear to perform better than those who may know the subject matter but are unable to effectively communicate.

After Betti's congressional hearing, I became convinced that we in DCMC should know where every defense contractor was on their program with respect to cost and schedule. I called every field commander to Washington—all 122 of them—and had them watch the tape of Betti's hearing. I then directed that within 30 days, they inform me about their program's status. This action became a high-water mark. It established DCMC as a viable source of timely information to the Secretary of Defense. We were in the contractor's plant, and we knew what the contractor was doing on the program. Now we had the discipline and an organization to push relevant information to the top. The fact that the under secretary now had access to this important information also tightened up the services' acquisition decisions. This was a first for DoD, which was well on its way to being able to effectively manage defense acquisition.

Thus the reorganization was complete. I felt good about what we had done. We had achieved Atwood's directive of improving the process. We had closed old organizations, established new ones, and conducted our personnel practices in a manner that gave maximum benefit and fairness to the employees. For the American taxpayer, we had reduced annual costs. I was privileged to have the opportunity to lead such a magnificent group in this effort and watch its success as we made decisions to accomplish our task. I also found it extremely satisfying to do something positive for the American taxpayer—something often talked about, but rarely achieved.

ORGANIZATIONAL LEADERSHIP

···

Key Elements of Change

I n forming a new command and working with senior defense acquisition leadership, I realized that
the way a leader interacts with people has a lot to
do with the result—both in mission performance and
interpersonal relationships. What follows is my impression of the dynamics of leadership in effective personnel
interaction while making major fundamental change
within organizations. Here, I suggest the key elements
of change that the leader must address to ensure success
in the new organization. In Part II, I look at important
actions and considerations related to the essential idea
of working within the organization. In Part III, I suggest
measures to ensure the individual development so necessary for successful leaders. These include actions that
both the leader and the subordinate can take. Part IV
contains a summary of the points made in the earlier
sections.

DETERMINING THE MISSION

I have noticed that some leaders begin a task without really understanding the objective. I believe it is important for leaders, in the beginning, to clearly form in their minds exactly what it is that the organization is to accomplish. In the final analysis, what will define success?

In the case of forming contract management within DoD, Atwood, in his mission statement, gave me a clear definition of what was to be accomplished. His charge was that we consolidate all contract administration into one command. We would streamline, avoid duplication, eliminate redundancy, and otherwise improve the process. These actions gave the entity a clear purpose. I soon concluded that if all personnel are focused on a single path and a clear goal, then the task becomes easier and success follows.

This idea of determining at the outset what exactly to do may sound simple, but it is vital to the ultimate success of everything that the leader later attempts. Organizations are designed to follow a path. Once a vision is stated, and once the organization is formed around that vision, changing it becomes difficult. This fact is both good and bad. Leaders, in establishing a vision, need to know clearly what it is that the organization should accomplish. They must then be able to explain it to all members of the organization. Once the organization understands and accepts the vision, it takes a life of its own. However, when leaders set the organization on the wrong track, they have to work hard to redirect it. Thus, the leader's vision is important and is a prerequisite to future success.

A relatively simple, but equally important, function that affects the definition of mission is to develop a deliberate, genuine concern for the health and welfare of employees in the organization. People will work to keep the organization alive and functioning along the leader's stated purposes if their basic needs are met. The synergism of the organization is a big dividend when the leader expresses a genuine concern for the people at the outset. I believe it is paramount to future success. And it means the mission will not be to eliminate people.

In establishing DCMC, I was fortunate that I was not asked to execute the normal government reorganizational downsizing. My mission statement said streamline, eliminate redundancies, and improve the organization. I believe the drafters of the original intent probably failed to add "and take out the money," but what often happens in government organizations when they reorganize is that the major focus becomes reducing cost first and then reorganizing around what is left. I concluded that leaders who focus on first reducing the cost, make bad decisions about the organization because the purpose is not clearly defined. It goes without saying that if an organization and its leadership concentrates solely on reducing cost, all other factors become secondary. It is then difficult to make an investment decision that allows some up-front money now to reduce the cost **later**. Those people who are watching and controlling the money will argue against that up-front investment because it will cost more for the current year.

I firmly believe that if those who count the money are the final decision-making authority, the leader is in trouble. This is not to say that those who count money are not good people who work very hard for the organization, nor does it mean that they are not team players. It just means that the leader will be forced to make decisions for the short term, compromising the long-term effects of investment planning.

When cost is not the first focus, the issue of taking care of people within the organization becomes paramount. To illustrate—in the process of closing five subordinate headquarters, we started with ten similar offices. We had deputies in each of the ten locations, but we were going to have jobs for only five of the individuals. The question was—who would end up in these five jobs? What would we do with the other deputies? These were the senior executives within the organization. I found that until I worked the issues of what was going to happen to these people, I was not going to get any substantial work from them on other organizational matters. It became apparent that each of these deputies spent a lot of time telephoning the others and talking about their career probabilities and possibilities. Only after deciding to address the personal concerns of these individuals was I able to move forward to reorganize contract management. I reasoned that if I had that kind of reaction from the seniors, those who were most eligible to retire, what kind of reaction would I get from the individual in mid-career?

I concluded that in organizational changes, one must establish a procedure that honestly and fairly addresses the people involved. I call it "take care of them." It's not coddling, but being concerned about people. Once people feel that the senior leadership is concerned about their health, welfare, and well-being; they coalesce around the leader's vision. This principle became so paramount to my way of thinking in developing a new organizational structure, that its absence would have doomed me to failure. In our case, I was lucky. Not faced with a stated requirement to reduce cost, but only to streamline; I was in a position to tell people that if they wanted to continue working, then I was willing to guarantee each person a job—but I would choose their employment location. They had two choices: take it, or quit. But the choice was theirs. This option is better than most reorganizations where the employee is simply terminated.

Since everybody knew he or she would have a job, organizational managers acted differently than they had in the past. We put the pressure on the managers and denied them the authority to bring in new people until the present employees had jobs. Managers could not hire people from outside the organization until they had first determined if anybody already employed in the organization wanted the job. To do this, we had to go beyond the normal personnel practices. The significance here was that subordinate leaders who normally said "this is a personnel function" were now required to get into the front end of the process and work with the personnel department. They had to say to the whole organization, "Here is a job. Is there anybody presently employed in the organization (worldwide) who would like to have it?" The process worked. Employees responded by taking these job offers. Putting the pressure on the managers implied that we must reorganize and reduce personnel numbers, which ultimately became the issue. In the end, we terminated the employment of only a handful of people out of a 20,000-person work force.

GETTING EMPLOYEE "BUY IN"

After the leader has defined the mission and given a clear vision of the expectations for the future, the next element for success within the organization is to get employees to "buy in." In large bureaucracies, when the employees resist change, leaders find themselves working to constantly over come employee resistance. They spend more time on such efforts than on accomplishing the mission. When the magic of employee acceptance occurs, the whole process takes on a life of its own; and the employees themselves find ways to make cultural change a reality. The key to getting employees to buy in is communication: direct, forceful, complete, and incessant. A. J. Stinnett defines communication in an organization as the "free exchange of information." One should not underestimate the fundamental importance of this particular phenomenon.

By nature, people tend to resist change. Generally, if a new leader takes over a job and presents a new predetermined organizational structure, the present organization will automatically resist. A leader who tries to force the change without obtaining the essential employee acceptance will experience what I call the "elastic approach." The leader can push it and pull it to the farthest extremes; however, as soon as the pressure lets up, the elastic retracts the function back to its original position. The employees will revert to performing as they did before. If employee behavior is to change, employees must think differently about their jobs. Otherwise, any change is temporary and illusory.

To illustrate, when Betti decided to create the new contract management command, he elected to place the command under DLA as a major subordinate command. The issue at the time was whether the Navy, Air Force, and Army would be subordinate to DLA. If the armed services had come to DLA for acquisition approval, then the Defense Department would have had a prescription for anarchy. The parochial feelings of the services were very strong; and we discovered, mostly by accident, that if we were going to create a new way of managing contracts, our mission must also be to create a totally new organization. Success would not be to simply merge the services to the new command.

We elected to take the best from each of the services, both in people and ideas. We stated that all who joined had equal personnel rights. This proved to be a most important decision. When assigning jobs, we did not assign the best jobs to those employed in DLA and allow those from the services to be placed in lesser jobs. We assigned people based upon merit to jobs without respect to where they had worked in the past. Only when we demonstrated conclusively that this would be the predominate policy did we get employee acceptance. Employees felt that they were part of a new beginning.

To accomplish this personnel equality, we created a structure that allowed anybody to submit what they considered a "best practice." An individual would offer a suggestion on how a certain task should be accomplished, and the DCMC leadership would look at the effectiveness of the approach. It was okay for the employee to say "this is how we did it back in my old organization." We organized a standing committee to look at this proposal and determine whether or not it would be beneficial and more economical if DCMC adopted the procedure. Obviously, however, one couldn't just take what the other service was doing and implement it into the new structure. So, even though an individual would come with a "best practice," there had to be some accommodation to give it the flexibility to be adapted to the way we were now operating.

An example of a practice we adopted was the Air Force's performance assessment reviews. The Air Force called them Contractor Operation Reviews (COR). If a contractor was having problems in contract performance, the contract management group would dispatch a team of professionals to review the operation and report deficiencies. This report would help both the contractor and the government's contract administration element in determining exactly what was wrong and where change was needed. The problem with the Air Force's system was that it established the work on a yearly schedule. The Air Force then told the contractors it was going to come in with 50 people in the next six to eight months for an extensive review, write a report, and assign a numerical grade. It was, in effect, a big inspection to the contractor. Contractors, of course, would work to place themselves in the best possible light. When they were notified of the forthcoming inspection they would hire consultants to give them a mini-review so they could correct problems before the official review. They would spend thousands of dollars preparing for the inspection!

The Air Force system was good, but it needed to be fine-tuned before we in a new contract management environment could accept it. So we changed the concept substantially. We explained to the contractor community that we would only give a contractor 30 days' notice. Our intent was to perform an advisory service to determine where problems existed and identify the predominant issues. We did not want them to spend a lot of money getting ready for a big inspection. Most importantly, we told the defense industry that we would give them the results and enough time to correct any problems. We would also try to keep knowledge of any corrected actions at the lowest level possible. (That proved hard when top Pentagon people and congressional staffers found out we were going into certain contractor facilities.) We adopted the Air Force's COR category as a base structure, and then modified it to meet the new requirements. We called it the Performance Assessment Review. This new procedure worked very well for both industry and the government.

Treating people equally became a lasting success. Devising a way for employees to tell us how they did it in their old organizations, and reviewing and implementing good ideas, boosted morale and proved beneficial to the overall goal.

EMPOWERING THE PEOPLE

It's always exciting to watch people getting really enthusiastic about their jobs. When they do, they work even better than expected. Empowering people makes this happen. Over the years, I have observed people performing by rote. The organization says we'll do it this way—these are the policies, the procedures, the rules, and the regulations. These pre-existing directives tend to stifle initiative. But when the leader comes out and purposely establishes a way for individuals to make decisions about their own job and performance, they feel comfortable with the process. The organization takes on an entirely different atmosphere. The result is surprising. No other single organizational issue has impressed me more than the concept: "Empower the people, and let them work from that empowerment." This technique pays a handsome dividend.

For this to happen, however, leaders must be comfortable with their own methods of operation. Leaders unsure of themselves and unwilling to take risks or let go of power (or perceived authority) will find the option of empowering people totally unacceptable.

Within an organization, the leader who wants to empower people must ensure that the subordinate supervisors do not act contrary to the leader's desires. It is not enough for leadership to say, "I hereby empower people." Employees are used to leadership talk and little action. They are also used to organizational changes that have no meaning. When a new leader arrives, an organization will be subjected to some form of organizational change. This change does not empower people. At best, it is merely a transition from one manager to another. To be successful, leaders must ensure that the organization itself understands that there has been a major new direction and that empowering people will be the norm. Then, they must check to ensure compliance.

An example: When we were reorganizing contract management, I asked the quality assurance division how many intermediate layers of supervisors were between me, the organizational head, and the individual quality assurance inspector on the contractor's floor. The answer from the staff was 11. Eleven intermediate layers of supervisors, all perceiving that they had the authority to make policy. Is it any wonder that employees in such organizations find it difficult to move in one direction?

I have learned that if leaders are going to make permanent, important changes to the organization, they must exhibit a genuine concern for the well-being of the employee. It is one thing to be appointed the leader, it is another to be truly the leader. People will follow effective leadership. People will tolerate for some time the ineffective appointed leader. While you should not pamper employees or be passive to the work force, great leaders will genuinely presume that their decisions are predicated on what is good for the individual. The synergy that comes about when the work force senses a leader is concerned about them is extremely valuable. It is more than one person can develop, and it is certainly more than one person can demand from an authority position. Authority comes in two forms: position of the job and acceptance by the organization. Successful leaders learn that a genuine concern for people is good both for the organization and for them personally.

It is not a great revelation to say that leaders come in various sizes, shapes, and forms with different individual philosophies about how to accomplish their objectives. My experience over the years shows that leaders fall into two categories: the "fire-eating dragons," who feel that they must push subordinates and that only they know the answers to all problems, and "benevolent leaders," who believe that people will rise to great expectations if empowered with a clear objective, authority, and responsibility.

I have observed both sides of leadership. In one case, I was aware of a very senior Army officer whose total approach to leadership was to induce fear. He was intelligent, but demanding. He knew the answers to all the issues, and subordinates would never measure up to his "standards." He would demand a response to his every whim, and he was so devoid of individual compassion that employee performance reports were demeaning. It was hard to find a subordinate who could please him. In spite of all this, the individual achieved the rank of lieutenant general.

While serving on a promotion board for Army officers, I read his reports on his officers. In every report that bore his signature, he cited some major wrong. I could not believe that everyone could be that wrong or bad in the job. His negative performance appraisals raised a question in my mind about the general himself. How could this individual be so successful if everyone who worked for him had a serious flaw?

I do not believe that this type of individual can achieve true greatness. People in organizations will suffer this type of personality for a time; and, when the individual ultimately departs, the employees give a party in honor of the departure. The irony is that this type of leadership behavior is contrary to military teaching and is ultimately ineffective. It does point out to organizations that, despite trying to effect a perfect personnel promotion system, the system sometimes breaks down and a "bad apple" gets through to promotion. I do not believe, however, that this occurs on a regular basis, and those who wish to adopt a leadership style as they are moving up in their careers would do well **not** to emulate this type behavior. Many individuals' careers were cut short because they exhibited the "I'm great and you are not" attitude.

In fact, I recall one instance when a senior official was selecting an individual for an important job. I had firsthand knowledge of the performance of an officer who was in the running for the job. The senior official had reports that the individual abused his employees. He asked me whether this was true. Although I was unaware of this trait, the senior official said he could not take the chance and hired another person. (Years later the person in question would retire from the Army in disgrace because he displayed abusive, noncaring personal traits.) Abusing subordinates has no positive effect on the organization at any time.

As a second lieutenant, I learned two things early: accomplish your mission and take care of the troops. That very basic

concept was instilled into every leader in the 1950s, and I have
found that it works well from lieutenant to general.

One of the best examples of a benevolent leader is Lieutenant
General Donald Babers. Babers had been a director of DLA. I had
the good fortune to serve as his chief of staff in 1984-85.
Observing his leadership style, I concluded that one could work
issues very hard but also be easy on people. I recall one incident
when DLA inadvertently released derogatory information that
was potentially embarrassing to the Secretary of Defense. Babers
was away from his office on travel; and when this information
became public, some in the Pentagon were incensed. They
wanted to know who had released the information. I received the
Pentagon's phone call, and the attitude was that they wanted
"somebody's head." I knew we were in trouble.

I contacted Babers by phone, informed him of the problem,
and told him that there were those in the Pentagon who were
extremely unhappy over the information release. Before knowing all the facts, Babers calmly called his Pentagon boss, took
full responsibility for the situation, and promised to fix the
problem. Afterwards, he instructed me to "gather the people
who know anything about this, and when I get back we'll work
the issue." I felt that Babers would come back mad and certainly
punish those responsible. I was surprised. He walked in, said
that he had talked to his boss at the Pentagon, and that they
were upset with us. He said, "Tell me how this happened." After
hearing the details, he said, "We need to learn how to handle
this in the future. It's not a big problem. Everybody go back to
work. I'll take care of the rest." A class act! Babers handled his
business dealings with people to the point that they always felt
good about themselves and about Babers.

The contrast between the two types of leaders is remarkable.
A leader who wants to know what is truly happening within the
organization has to create a climate that genuinely fosters interest in issues and not abuse of people. Then, and only then,
will people feel comfortable enough to tell the leader what is really going on.

If employees feel that their job is in jeopardy, they will work
to protect the job. The leader must be able to create a climate

where people feel they can openly discuss change, change that would benefit the organization.

Dr. W. Edwards Deming, the guru of quality management, said it best. "If you always do what you've always done, you'll always get what you've always gotten." Organizations, once established, will continue with a procedure until something happens to cause a change. Many subordinates will mouth polite acceptance to making change, but what happens is that too often they go to staff meetings, go through the motions of acceptance, but don't embrace the concept of changing what they have been doing.

It is the leader's responsibility to set the organizational climate. Employees must feel confident about themselves, the leader, and the organization before they will accept change. If a leader leads with fear, the employee will feel threatened, and organizational changes will be difficult.

CREATING A SENSE OF URGENCY

One of the best tools in a leader's kit is the ability to set the tone for the organization. Organizations need to have a sense of direction and timing. In the military, a unit with a good sense of timing has esprit de corps. Simply stated, this unit is focused and purposeful. It knows where it is going, and it will know when it gets there. A sense of urgency instills into the organization a commitment to get on with the issues. It implies that there is a goal and a time to achieve this goal. In military planning, you do not start prosecuting a war without feeling you can ultimately win. The same applies to a business organization. If an organization is given a task without a time limit, lethargy sets in, and the organizational bureaucracy will churn the issue, never allowing for a conclusion.

Organizations want to be led. They like to have the feeling of accomplishment, and one of the ways that they can get that feeling is for the leader to put a "mark on the wall," and say, "I want us to be at this point on this date." When it is done properly, the organization will coalesce around that date, and subordinate leaders will predicate their plans based upon the target objective. It is also the bold stroke of the leader who can create a sense of urgency in the organization.

To illustrate the importance of creating urgency, consider what happened in 1988 shortly after I assumed the job as deputy director for acquisition management of DLA. I had served many years in contract management and felt I knew the business from apprentice to journeyman. For many years I was of the opinion that, in managing government contracts, the government knew about the contractor's performance history. However, this information never got to those making new procurement decisions. The truth was that the government often failed to keep "book" about the contractor's past performance, and no one could tell contracting officers what they needed to know prior to awarding future contracts. This does not mean that the government does not keep records, but it appeared that only one segment of the government would keep records about a contractor and often would not tell the other segments what they needed to know.

It seemed to me that with all the sophisticated computer industry technology, the government should be able to devise a system that would allow truthful and factual contractor performance information to be projected to any contracting officer in government. Contracting officers would then make awards only to those who had performed well on previous contracts. Nice thought; an idea which, to me, would increase the efficiency of government contracting immeasurably. It would allow contracting officers to know the responsiveness and the responsibility of those who had done business with the government previously; and it would allow contracting officers to make the determination, which is their responsibility, to only deal with good contractors and, correspondingly, to weed out those contractors who did not perform. This would save the taxpayer money and improve administration of defense contracts.

In July 1988, I directed what I thought was a very simple organizational task. I asked the staff to design a computer software program that would collect information in one central place so that any contracting officer in the government would be able to access information on a contractor's performance.

Contracting officers awarding new contracts would be able to find out whether the contractor previously delivered on time and with acceptable quality.

Four years later and with all my urging, I still did not have this simple program implemented. My failure? In 1988 I did not establish a sense of urgency. I wrongly assumed that the organization, once accepting what I wanted, would move out and quickly accomplish the task. No one said to me, "This is not what we're going to do," but organizations often get busy on other projects and fail to move toward completion of one. That happened in this case.

First the staff put a program manager in charge and gathered a lot of smart people to study the concept. Then they added more people and tasks to the point that, when they did give me the first review, it was so cumbersome, complicated, and laden with extra baggage that it was incapable of working. The final cost was enormous. The end result would be a bloated bureaucracy that could not work the issue successfully. I disapproved. Then I directed the staff to return with a simpler plan. This process occurred three more times in four and one half years. What we had was a jobs program. Many smart people were gainfully employed on a project that had the "general's" personal interest. I put money in the budget to support the effort, but I had failed to create a sense of urgency with the staff. We had no time limit to bring this project to a close.

I finally understood the urgency issue that organizations must have. The leader should pick a person to be in charge, tell the organization when the project is to be completed, and hold the organization accountable for meeting that date. I ultimately picked June 1992 as the date that this program was to be accomplished. That date was a year away from the decision. The organization made great progress toward the goal, but when I left in November 1992, they were just beginning to implement the program, almost five years after first receiving the project.

The failure was in my management. I had established the vision. I had put money into the project. But, I left it to the organization to decide how much and when. I underestimated the complexity, and most importantly, I failed to induce the sense of urgency that is required for success.

On the other hand, in the contract management reorganizations, we established five headquarters during the month of August 1990 and were able to create a sense of urgency that enabled the organization to do things very quickly.

Sometimes situations dictate a sense of urgency. During this same period, the United States prepared for and fought the Gulf War in the Middle East, Desert Shield/Desert Storm. I was the senior acquisition executive for DLA and responsible for the wholesale procurement of all of the food for the military services. Before the war started, I was in the Pentagon one morning at 6:30 a.m. I was informed that President Bush had directed an increase in the troop strength in the Persian Gulf from 200,000 to 400,000 troops as rapidly as possible. I have often joked that the President didn't ask me about this decision. He assumed, or no one suggested otherwise, that there would be enough food to provide 1.2 million meals a day. The military feeding plan for troops in combat consisted of tray packs. (Tray packs are like cafeteria food in metal trays, with a removable top. They are heated in hot water and will feed up to 18 people.) Combat rations were "meals ready to eat" (MREs), a type of freeze-dried product that can be heated in the pouch and immediately consumed. Both these food products are peculiar to the military. Civilians do not generally consume them, so the United States' industrial base comprised about three producers for MREs and six producers/assemblers for the tray packs. At the time the President decided to increase troop strength, all producers were operating at maximum capacity.

The desired food for soldiers in garrison (base camp) is called "A" rations. This type of meal is the same as one would eat in a restaurant—a hot meal, prepared over a stove. The soldiers in Desert Shield were being fed "A" rations. When combat actions start, and armies are on the move, units do not stop and prepare food, they consume already prepared meals. This is the intent of the combat ration; and, thus, the Army and industry invented tray rations and MREs.

After receiving the President's directive to increase troop strength from 200,000 to 400,000, I went back to the DLA headquarters and assembled the "food" staff. I asked, "Can the U.S. industrial base support the requirement to feed 400,000 troops a day?" The answer was that we would be short about three million meals per month. Obviously, this would be disastrous. Here we had a nation preparing to go to war, with U.S. service men and women halfway around the world; and the U.S. Department of Defense would be unable to feed them their next meal. One can imagine the letters to the President of the United States castigating the administration and the military over this failure. Obviously, we had a situation that created a tremendous sense of urgency.

Our answer came from an experiment the Army had been conducting with prepared meals that could be microwaved. These were the kind that the diet industry (Weight Watchers, Jenny Craig, etc.) had developed for their programs. These meals contain around 300 calories each. They are small, individually packed meals that can be heated in many ways. They are in bright packaging (as opposed to the dark green of the Army). We later discovered that this increased soldier acceptance of the product. The Army Surgeon General and the Army's deputy chief of staff of logistics gave approval for the Army to use the product, and we contracted from companies such as Borden and Carnation (two of the largest producers of this type of food). The day following the presidential directive to increase troop strength, we placed letter contracts with industry for about $700 million—enough to provide the combat force with three million meals per month. (The American food industry was very responsive to the requirements of the military at war.)

All this illustrates the importance of urgency. To conclude, the process needs a sense of urgency. If urgency is not created through the circumstances, the leader must create it. The engine of the organization will function more smoothly with a completion date and a timetable. With clear guidance as to what is required, and a sense of urgency, the likelihood of success increases.

BASHING BUREAUCRACY

Bureaucratic processes become the norm in large-group behavior. Once the "standard operating procedure" becomes accepted, it is very difficult for a new idea to take hold. To facilitate change, the leader must create an atmosphere that allows and encourages bashing bureaucracies and must become the head cheerleader in this effort. Only when employees really question why things are done can change take place. All must understand that change is a permanent part of what they do and the way they do it. The leader establishes that it's okay to question what was done in the past; in fact, questioning is required to change the way things are done and increase efficiency for tomorrow. Creating an atmosphere for change is really instilling a desire to look realistically for things that can be improved. Leaders cannot determine everything that needs to be done. They need help, and the help must come from the work force. In the proper atmosphere, these changes, when implemented, will improve an organization's efficiency.

At one point, I asked the DCMC staff, "How many reports do we have that could be eliminated?" The answer came back, "None. They're all needed." The command was spending approximately $1 million a year on paper alone. I could not believe that all the reports were useful. When I questioned the people who used the reports, they felt threatened. I then said, "I am not going to eliminate jobs, I just want to know how we can save money on paper." The answer came back, "twenty percent," with recommendations on which reports to eliminate. Even at that, I do not believe that we eliminated all the unneeded reports. But, then, the issue is how to get people in the organization to help the leader streamline. I believe that people want to be a part of a vibrant and efficient organization. They want to eliminate waste, but they must be secure in their jobs first. So, the leader must establish a climate that spurs the work force to really look at practices and decide how to eliminate unnecessary tasks.

PRESENTING A CLEAR VISION

All bureaucracies, whether government or business, tend to staff their organizations with people who like to complicate matters. The more an issue is worked, the more detailed and complicated it becomes. The successful leader must be able to reduce complicated matters to simple terms. General Eisenhower, in leading the Allied Forces to victory in World War II, was given a mission that stated in part, "You will enter the continent of Europe." There was no doubt what he was charged to do. I think one of the major issues today is for leaders to present clear mission statements to the work force in simple terms that define exactly what the organization needs to accomplish. I have already stressed this in the first key element of change, but this element goes beyond that.

To be successful, organizations must have a vision—a direction. Without this there can be no organizational success. In addition, the leader must draw the organization close through cooperation from individual members. Through this closeness, they will concentrate on the issues and vision. In building DCMC, we knew we wanted to consolidate and reduce to five headquarters. The vision was to be the best, most affordable contract administration service organization in the world by turning contract commitments into quality products and services. Using this vision, we drew almost 20,000 people together to focus on one common cause.

But, a clear vision is only the first step. The leader must define expectations up front and early in the process, addressing both positive and negative consequences. This forces discipline onto the organization, both on the employees and on the leader personally. The leader must know what is expected of the employees. Industry uses management by objectives or "bottom line." Government and bureaucracies do not relate to a profit-and-loss statement, although they should. In a nonprofit organization, the leader must define those subsets that are a substitute for a profit-and-loss-statement. Leaders must define what the organization does well, and what it does poorly. The answers to these questions will determine what is expected in the future.

In DCMC, we knew we were going to consolidate and streamline from 26,000 people to some undefined number. Fortunately, we were able to offer challenging and rewarding jobs to most. Unfortunately, this did not happen without some employee pain. There would not be jobs for all 26,000 initial employees. Those who wanted to continue employment with us would be required to make career decisions to move to a new location, take a job in another organization, or take a reduction in pay to a lesser job. Others would retire if eligible or terminate employment. Our leadership task was to create the proper climate to allow for easier employee decisions. Together, as employees and management, we studied the issue. I believe in the end this method proved beneficial to the employees.

If the leader is forthright and honest about the agenda, I believe people will respond positively. Conversely, when employees feel the leadership is dishonest and withholding information, speculation begins, which leads to distrust. A leader who establishes truth, honesty, integrity, and open communication within an organization from the outset builds a solid foundation for future management-employee relationships.

BUILDING FOR A FINAL DECISION

I believe the preferred way to make policy is not at the point of decision, but at a point much earlier. To an observer, it appears that when organizations are making major decisions, they do so at big meetings. A large group of people sits around a table, talking and agreeing. Then the leader decides.

Decisions are certainly made at these meetings, but what precedes them is critical to the outcome. Typically, a middle management action officer charged with developing the facts, opposing courses of action, and assumptions will discuss the issues and present a conclusion. Then the staff agrees on a recommendation for the leader to accept. The key player is the action officer, who initiates the process. The action officer's conclusions will determine to a large measure the final outcome. Of course, the final decision is made by the decision-maker, but it is the action officer who sets the tone of the action.

In the Pentagon, majors and lieutenant colonels refer to this process as "making their generals smart." This is not to say that the generals have no say on the issue. What normally transpires is that, if there is an issue whose outcome can be determined "either way," the person crafting the staffing document is the one determining the direction of the decision.

A leader with a keen interest in the subject matter or the final outcome should hold an early planning session. This meeting should be used to guide the staff on the recommended course of action. When the subject is truly open for discussion and the leader has no disposition to the final outcome, then the staff should be told. My experience indicates that in the absence of specific guidance, staff officers will recommend the best course of action consistent with past management decisions. Leaders who wish to change the thinking of the past must assert themselves early in the process to give the staff new direction. Otherwise, the recommendation will be geared to past management practices. To be a change agent, make the major leadership contribution before the action officer draws conclusions and publishes the findings.

PART II

ORGANIZATIONAL LEADERSHIP

Working Within the Organization

BAD NEWS DOES NOT IMPROVE WITH AGE

Lieutenant General Woodrow Vaughn taught me the adage that bad news never improves with age. While that may be a profound statement when dealing with the issues, one also has to recognize that a leader must actively establish a positive climate to allow subordinates to communicate bad news. That is what we did with the "bell ringer" program at DCMC, as described earlier. Employees must feel that the leader will accept bad news without "shooting the messenger." However, employees must realize that when they deliver bad news; they should, if time permits, offer a recommended solution.

In those cases where the organization has a failure, it is difficult to get employees to immediately admit the failure to the leader. The natural tendency is for the employees to work to reduce the damage. But often, recovery is beyond the subordinate employee's ability to solve alone. The leader who establishes the climate that bad news should be forwarded immediately is in a much better position to solve the problem. It has been my experience that the longer bad news sits, the worse it gets. (We are not discussing transgressions by fellow employees. In these cases it seems everyone wants to tell the boss the other person's failure.)

In the late 1970s, the Army assigned me to Fort Lee, Virginia, to work for Major General Fred C. Sheffey, the first African-American officer ever to command Fort Lee. I was his officer in charge of community affairs. Sheffey was coming to the end of his military career and, during the annual Black History Week, he invited the president of his former college (an historically black college) to be the featured speaker at the Black History Week celebration.

At the time, the officer's club was losing money, and I was preoccupied trying to manage the club back to profitability. This preoccupation with club profits and the inability to properly prioritize my work resulted in an embarrassing failure.

Fort Lee's Black History Week celebration lasted two days. The first day went flawlessly. The college president made a marvelous speech to a packed audience at the quartermaster school. The next day he was to appear at the post chapel for a final speech before he departed.

It was Fort Lee's custom for this of type post event that battalion commanders would ensure that 40 to 50 soldiers were in the seats. The post had five battalions, and each filling their quota of seats made a nice crowd for a visiting speaker. I had been a battalion commander and was aware of this custom. At this time, many battalion commanders were new to the job and did not know of the 50-soldier requirement. In my concern over the officer's club profitability, I did not ensure that these battalions were filling their "allotted" seats in the post chapel. The hour for the general and college president to arrive was approaching.

I arrived 15 minutes before the scheduled event to find only four people in the large auditorium! I knew immediately what had happened. The battalions had failed to schedule their participation. What an embarrassment! I immediately scrambled to get people to fill the seats. We delayed the event almost an hour to allow the transportation of soldiers to the post chapel. Meanwhile, the general and his guest waited until we were able to assemble a proper crowd. I felt that the organization had let the general down, especially when he asked me, "Chuck, how could this have happened?" Well, it was each battalion commander's responsibility to ensure that the seats were occupied, but I was in charge of community affairs. While it is hard to pin blame, one thing is for sure—this was a classic example of bad staff planning.

Bad news does not improve with age. Neither Sheffey nor I talked about this after the event (until 16 years later). In retrospect, I should have gone to him and discussed the matter rather than assuming he knew what had happened and who was at fault. I had become so involved in all the details that the obvious was overlooked. The incident taught me a valuable lesson. For the rest of my military career, I always took the attitude that if there is bad news, go immediately to the leader and discuss the situation. It is always better to deal with the issues than with the innuendos and hurt feelings that accompany something that goes wrong. I used to joke to my subordinates, "Bring the issue while there is still some life left in the problem so I can work it back to health."

DON'T SHOOT THE MESSENGER

Next to being able to accept bad news gracefully, the leader should be gentle on subordinates. I find it interesting that some leaders become screamers, shouters, and employee abusers. I know of no other single character trait that chills and dampens the response of subordinates more than having a boss with a reputation of "shooting the messenger" of bad news. When this happens, organizational productivity always suffers. From time to time, all organizations experience events that are not as pleasant as the leader would like. That is to be expected. Leaders must recognize that if they are going to be effective, they must create the climate that allows a subordinate to walk in and say, "We've got a problem," without fearing execution on the spot.

Lieutenant General (later promoted to General) Jimmy Ross, then deputy chief of staff for logistics for the U.S. Army, was the type of officer that could accept bad news with grace. After listening to the problem, he would often say, "Alright, let's work the issue." His actions put people around him at such ease that they greatly admired him and would follow him anywhere.

During the height of Desert Shield and Desert Storm (1991), Ross was leading the logistical effort to supply a half million troops halfway around the world. The number of issues and problems that arose on a daily basis was enormous. The staff would meet each morning at 7:00 a.m. to assess the previous day's efforts. Not once in the 8 months' of the military operation did I hear him raise his voice at a subordinate despite numerous problems, a tight schedule, and all of us feeling a great amount of stress. Ross considered each issue on merit and always preserved individual integrity. He was truly a great officer who would immediately confront anything negative and dispense with it quickly. I know of no other Army general who was as consistent in separating the bad news of the issue from the people who were involved with the issue. He was very accomplished in his dealings with both issues and people, and he was immensely successful.

LIFE IS NOT A POPULARITY CONTEST

Every leader knows that tough decisions will arise. The axiom, life is not a popularity contest, is certainly applicable to the organizational leader. In dealing with day-to-day issues, leaders will face much opposition, and the ones who try to make decisions based on popularity will often find trouble. My advice is to go for the percentage; establish a few Sunday-school values that pay off. The leader who resolves at the outset to treat everyone with dignity, fairness, and equality and expresses a genuine concern for the whole organization, not just the favored pets, will find work life easier.

Of course, decisions centered around these simple elements will, at times, force the leader to make unpopular decisions. But they will be just and fair decisions. Ultimately, the employees may complain, but individuals will concede, "I don't like the decision, but I respect fairness." Employees will stand behind the leader who can make unpopular, yet fair, decisions that uphold the good of the organization without preferentially treating a favored few. My experience has been that, regardless of how well intended decisions might be, a leader must rigorously adhere to the simple principle of fairness.

I learned this during the early 1970s when I was assigned to the contract administration organization in Atlanta, Georgia. There, I met Malcolm Dean, a strong supporter of Martin Luther King, Jr.'s, civil rights movement. Then commander Colonel Edward B. Turner noticed Dean's commitment to equal and civil rights and eventually hired him as the equal employment opportunity officer for the organization. I soon developed the greatest regard for his ability to negotiate issues. He taught me that one has to give and take in negotiations, that one gives a little today to win more tomorrow, and that your "going-in position" must always be right and just. Dean could be dogmatic in his pursuit of his goal, but he was a very gifted negotiator. I attribute any success I later developed as a contract negotiator to the lessons I learned first-hand from hours of negotiating with Dean on the equal employment issues. The most important of these issues was that the leader must look at the whole organization, base decisions on the good of the whole, and not be swayed by impacts on individuals. As Mr. Spock of the popular television program/movie, "Star Trek," says, "The needs of the many outweigh the needs of the few or the one."

Regarding union negotiations, I have found that no matter how well intended leaders are, simultaneously pleasing every element they represent is impossible. In negotiations on the contract administration reorganization (DCMC), the union leadership did not want any jobs impacted. After all, their basic charter is to preserve jobs, often at any price. Negotiation is very difficult when one side is so extreme and unwilling to give at least a little. When two diametrically opposed factions come together (the organizational need for change versus the union's mandate to retain jobs), ultimately one side will have to give.

Unfortunately, it is the classic case of win-lose. If the union wins on no job loss, there will be no organizational change. If management wins and jobs are lost, the union loses. In contract negotiations, concessions must be made for the benefit of both parties. The test of fairness to the most people is absolutely essential. The best case in these negotiations is for both sides to take a small victory. The union can acknowledge that there will be jobs that are not needed and can be eliminated; management proposes to offer the displaced employees priority to position

transfers, more time on the payroll before separation, early retirement, etc. The key is that each side have empathy for the
other's position.

The guiding principles for both union and management
should be respect for fairness, equality, and improving overall
employee morale. The leader cannot make decisions based
upon popularity, nor be removed from the fact that decisions
that affect the lives of working people are immensely important.
Therefore, an earnest attempt to make decisions based upon
fairness is absolutely a prerequisite for effective leadership.

BE ETHICALLY DRIVEN

The leader who is ethically driven and adheres to what is
right will find the next day better than the person who tries to
walk the narrow ledge without falling off. A supreme court justice when asked, "How far to the edge can I walk and still be
legal?" replied, "I don't know, but I can certainly tell you how
far back to walk and be in good shape." Ethics, leadership, and
management go hand in hand. A leader cannot take the attitude
of "do as I say, not do as I do."

A great Army general and personal mentor, Lieutenant
General Benjamin Register, was the type of individual who lived
the "do as I do" principle. He conducted his life as though it was
to be portrayed on the front page of the newspaper. In fact,
Register was so well regarded in ethical leadership principles
that years after army retirement, he was giving advice to a corporation on how to develop its corporate ethics plan. The government representative charged with reviewing corporate ethics
plans had known Register and his reputation for many years.
Upon learning that Register advised the corporation, she told
me before reviewing the plan, "I imagine that this will be one of
the best and most comprehensive plans that I have reviewed."
She later reported to me that it was. I believe a leader can be
truly great only if ethically driven.

I have often thought the benchmark for right and wrong
boils down to the question, "Can I adequately explain this to

my mother?" Leaders who consistently pass that test will find that their decisions will keep them out of trouble.

When ethics are put aside, it is the small things that trap one on the way to the larger goal: the individual who misappropriates government vehicles for personal use, the presidential candidate who conducts illicit sexual liaisons, the individual who lies to a grand jury on even small issues. These infractions work against the larger issue of individual ethics. The question becomes whether one can believe the individual, whether the perception of trust is evident.

Contrast the public perception of the ethically driven leader to the senior government official who is arrested and charged with shoplifting. While the crime is a misdemeanor under the law, the damage to the individual's reputation is catastrophic. One small indiscretion can wipe out a lifetime of earning the people's confidence in your ability to be truthful and reliable. The leader who loses the people's perception of trustworthiness and reliability loses all, including the respect of those he or she wishes to lead.

By simply adhering to the "can I explain this to my mother" principle, I sleep well at night. Worry about the actions and decisions of the previous day are eliminated! In organizations, leaders must make many daily decisions, any of which can come back to haunt them later. It is impossible to remember every action to ensure that one is not "walking against the edge." How much better to make decisions that allow a sufficient distance from the edge than to take the chance of stumbling and falling.

THE BIG BANG THEORY

Organizations evolve slowly and operate slowly. The larger they get, the more bureaucratic they become—standard operating procedures, regulations, and rules by which the organization lives become cast in stone. Once a practice gets ingrained, it is hard for the leader to change it. I have found that, to change the corporate culture and direction, the leader should reduce the message to the employees to simple terms and repeat it often. It also helps to create a significant event and have a "big bang" as a result. This is what we did when we closed all the old DCAST Regions and opened new offices in the same month. Employees get used to things moving slowly, and when the leader speeds it up, results are positive.

Employees become jaded in organizational structures. They are used to organizational politics and leaders coming and going. Each time the organization gets a new leader, there is a flood of new ideas. When employees observe various leaders over the course of time, they grow accustomed to this type of leadership change. Often no progress is made; and, after time, the leader settles in, and the organization returns to the old way of doing things. The more one is exposed to new ways of doing things, the more resistant one is to change. Organizational leaders must recognize that they are not the first new leaders to come to the organization and, in all probability, will not be the last. To command more than faint recognition for leadership direction requires understanding the environment.

We have discussed the merits of reducing complicated issues to simple terms and getting the employees to "buy in" to the new thinking. The leader must become a cheerleader and establish at the outset what to do and the course to follow. Enthusiastically repeating this statement of direction to the employees will create a climate of expecting great things. Lieutenant General Gus Pagonis, U.S. Army logistical hero of Desert Storm was especially adept in this manner. He had the ability to convince people that they should perform as he directed. The leader who can set the direction in clear, simple terms and then repeat that direction often will emerge as the successful leader. Repetition is crucial to a leader's message. For example, in the middle of the DCMC reorganization, I was on a trip to the operating elements. A mid-level employee said to me, "We know that this is important to you, for we read and hear from other locations where you have talked the same simple message. You are consistent in what you are asking us to do." Bingo! I thought, "Consistency, simplicity, and repetition—the leadership elements that produce action and success."

SUBSTANCE—NOT FORM

Having served as an Army general officer, I attended many briefings that required developing action plans to accomplish tasks. Attending these briefings, I became increasingly aware that most situations fall into one of two categories: those with substance and those based solely on form. Substance, of course, leads to a course of action. Form only makes the individual actor look good. In the latter case, there is often the illusion of success, but without substance, a plan will fail in execution.

I once was associated with an individual who would get ready for a tough task by sharpening his pencils, straightening papers on the desk to a certain angle, and ensuring that all the paper clips were pointed in the same direction. While it was obvious he was fiddling, it is surprising to me to finally realize how many people really feel they are advancing the issues while, in reality, they are promoting form over substance. It is the job of staff members to involve themselves in details. However, people often become so involved in process that they forget about content.

In the early 1960s in Saudi Arabia, I worked for Brigadier General Jerry Addington, who required subordinates to speak and write only in the active voice. He would always say, "John ate the apple." Never, "An apple was eaten by John." He forced the organization to focus on action-orientated situations and would demand that individuals talk only about substance. Instead of concentrating on the perception of performance, they were held accountable for what they were actually doing to accomplish their goals. Addington was a unique leader to say the least. He once directed several colonels to fly from Riyadh to Daharan to attend his "English lesson" so that they could learn to communicate in the active voice. While his methods were somewhat unorthodox, he would concentrate on substance and look for results from each encounter. To the subordinate who was pushing a particular task, this was a blessing. Here we had a senior leader who knew what the substantive issues and actions were. As a result, decisions would flow to the bottom rather rapidly, and the immediate level of supervisors between the action officer and the senior would have to have more than a passing knowledge about the issues. In the end, things got done.

The leader should always conclude a meeting by assigning a definite course of action. This process will keep the tension on the organization, and the group members will focus on substance.

KICK THE CAN

Sometimes senior managers have to make big issues out of small ones to get the group's attention. In 1978, commanding a battalion of young soldiers just entering the Army, I was intrigued by a consistent facet of human behavior; when these young soldiers had done something wrong, they could be very articulate in explaining why they did it. In administering non-judicial punishment for minor infractions, I would always ask the soldier what he or she had done and why. I received a wide variety of responses. If it appeared that I was buying into these "explanations," they could really lay it on and further convolute the issue as they tried to explain it.

One day as I was listening to a very articulate soldier "con" me, I noticed the waste paper basket adjacent to my chair. I thought, "He really thinks he is sucking me into this explanation." I played along for a moment, and then looked at him and said, "Soldier, I think you are playing me for a big sucker," and I got up and kicked the waste paper basket, making a loud noise. The soldier's expression indicated that I had made a telling point. It was startling. He immediately acknowledged his transgression and promised never to do it again. I gave him extra duty, and he left under the supervision of his sergeant. He was never back to see me for discipline again.

My purpose in administering the punishment was not to punish, but to change behavior. If the leader of a military unit can reduce incidence and raise soldier morale, then the unit will accomplish its intended mission. The unit that is victorious will be the unit with the best maintained equipment and the best soldier morale. I found that "kicking the can" was a surprise technique that would elicit positive response! Later, as I dealt with more mature individuals, I certainly could not "kick the can," but could use a variation of the technique as a leadership tool.

A decade later, I was working a very important organizational issue dealing with the question of where the responsibility for administering petroleum quality assurance lies in DoD. Quality inspectors all over the world were reporting back to the fuel purchasing headquarters in Washington. The change was to have these inspectors report to DCMC instead. Naturally, the old organization did not want to have any part of the change. In a meeting on the subject, everybody had strong opinions. Those representing the current organization did not want to relinquish any control over what they had done in the past. The deputy secretary of defense had directed a change, but no one was willing to make the first move. We were at an impasse.

I called another meeting of principals; and midway through this meeting, it became obvious that all we were going to accomplish was further stalling and polarization of each side's position. I stopped the meeting abruptly, got up, and announced to the fuel organization leader that I felt that the parties had not come with serious intent to negotiate—that they were being bureaucratic—and that we needed to go back and reexamine their position. When they were ready to move forward and negotiate in good faith, we would reconvene. I then walked out of the meeting.

The fuel organization leader, who was and is a friend, later confided to me that was a startling and embarrassing episode for him. He knew he had to lead the charge and that change would be coming. It was only a question of what the change was going to be. The previous meetings had contained an element of form—not substance. When he returned to his headquarters, he started working the issue with a serious intent to reach a conclusion. Later, he was a key player and very successful in formulating the change to the program.

A mature version of "kick the can" has all the element of surprise in tough negotiations. Sometimes the unexpected is required to get the organization to face the issues and move to more productive negotiations.

WOULD YOUR MOTHER BUY THIS?

The successful manager/leader must be able to take complex issues and reduce them to their simplest terms. The greatest test, as in the chapter "Be Ethically Driven," is whether your mother can buy into the principle. I've observed that too often organizations take smart, educated people who can work a complicated issue and end up making it so complex that no one of ordinary intelligence can understand what they are trying to accomplish. This is especially true with lawyers (I have been one for over 20 years) on legal issues, comptrollers on financial matters, and those in the relatively new career field of information services (those who design, develop, and operate information systems).

I discovered a leadership technique to solve the issue of complication vs. simplicity. I would say to the organization, "The meeting shall last no more than one hour; the briefer can use no more than five charts to explain meeting contents and the desired outcome. After each meeting, there will be a conclusion and a recommendation." This process forces one to concentrate on presenting complex issues in simple terms on a prescribed time line with a well-thought recommendation for action. It also helps the leader consolidate thoughts and simplify the issues in terms that nontechnical persons can understand.

Today's organizations are complex. No manager, regardless of background, will have the technical capability to know every facet of modern business. Leaders must develop a technique that allows them to present essential information clearly and understandably so that others can make intelligent, informed decisions.

THE 80-PERCENT RULE

Given a complicated issue, staff officers will study a problem indefinitely if the leader does not give deadlines. Action officers will continue to study, fine-tuning the issues until closure becomes nearly impossible. The more complicated the issue, the more this appears to be the case.

It is my experience that a leader who has grasped 80 percent of the relevant facts of an issue is ready for an informed and intelligent decision. Thus, I call this the 80-percent rule. By deciding at this point, the leader can save time, exploit the opportunity, and possibly capture the surprise element.

This does not mean that the leader should make arbitrary and capricious decisions. Nor does it mean merely looking for consensus within the group, although an effort toward consensus is always beneficial. But it does mean decisive action. The leader who has the decision-making authority and responsibility should recognize that there must be a limit to the discussion, and at some point action must be taken. The 80-percent rule has often worked for me in moving things along.

FASTER THAN A SPEEDING BULLET

Action must be taken. The 80-percent rule expedites reaching a decision. Then, there must be a plan to execute that decision. I advise executing with utmost speed by placing the organization into what I call a "lean forward in the foxhole" mode. Organizational members want to be led. They want to be decisively engaged in an operation that will produce results. They like to see progress. Too often decisions are made, and the plan for execution is left to others. The leader who decides to walk away without paying attention to the execution of a decision is making a very serious mistake. This follow-through on execution is as important as the quality of the decision.

As discussed in DCMC's plan for closure of five contract management regions in 1990, the organization had studied the issue and concluded that since we had 18 months to complete the task, the correct solution would be to close one region every three months. I felt there was no reason for an incremental execution, so I decided to close all in the month of August 1990. This caused an organizational surprise. However, once the organization got beyond this shock, the plan came together and the energy level that was created with moving out fast gave us momentum to successfully tackle other organizational issues.

So my recommendation to a leader is—once you have gathered the facts and made a decision, move to organize so the staff can implement that decision as quickly as possible. Pay as much attention to the who, what, where, and when of the execution as you did to making the decision. The combination of these two factors, along with a specific time to start and stop, will go a long way toward producing success.

THE NINE LIVES OF A BUREAUCRACY

I have observed that bureaucracies, whether in the government or the business world, will work to keep themselves alive. An organization that is no longer needed or one that has achieved its mission will rarely if ever come forward and say, "We're finished. What would you have us do now?" Once established, people in organizations, regardless of the intent, will work to keep themselves in a job. An exception may be when a commission is established with a specific time to start and a specific time to end. But here, I am talking about organizations that started out to be indefinite in nature. The leader must be mindful that even those who are trusted agents and are giving recommendations concerning other organizational matters are the same individuals who in the end will work to maintain their own interests. This should not come as any major surprise. Self-preservation is a very strong instinct.

In my role as deputy director at DLA, I had a small organizational section composed of very competent people whose purpose clearly had been achieved. Knowing that I was faced with a reorganizational challenge and also knowing that their purpose had been accomplished, they still went searching for a mission. They felt that they were excepted from reorganization. I came away from this experience understanding how strong the basic security factor of employment is. The leader must consistently reassure the work force that each person has security within the organization before suggesting that positions be abolished. I also came to understand that this reassurance is not possible unless the leader has identified other positions that are available so that the employee can see a logical progression to the next position. Once the individual security factor is satisfied, the leader can count on these individuals to help develop a change model.

A leader also must recognize that those who are close may not always provide the most essential and impartial advice. This is not because the individual wishes to be deceitful, but because the security factor will blind the employee to other options. In these cases, leaders must either take their own counsel or satisfy the security factor first and then work the change.

DO UNTO THE STAFF AS YOU WOULD HAVE THEM DO UNTO YOU

Some managers feel that they can only deal with the their immediate superior and ignore the boss's staff. This is a mistake. The subordinate leader should always remember that the superior's staff exerts a tremendous amount of authority. It is not always apparent; however, staff members have the constant ear of the superior. This alone places them in a position of being able to influence the agenda.

Subordinate managers will always have the opportunity to speak with the superior. However, subordinates often are removed from the superior's place of business. So, although the subordinate sees the superior when he comes to town, it is the staff that has the superior's constant ear. If the subordinate leader is not mindful of how to deal with the superior's staff and gets into a conflict with them, they will "eat the subordinate's lunch." This does not mean that one should "kowtow" to the superior's staff. Instead, work with them, and afford each a degree of courtesy and deference. Common courtesy should be the rule. If the subordinate leader is going to present a complex subject at next week's staff meeting, a phone call to the key staff officer with an advance copy of the charts and briefing will go a long way toward building good staff relationships. Most decisions are determined prior to the big meeting anyway (and should be, as already noted). The subordinate leader should work the superior's staff before introducing a major new issue.

In my experience, there is a direct correlation between the effort in preparing the staff to accept a new idea and the effort that it takes to receive the superior's support in the formal meeting. If the senior leader's staff does not accept the proposal, the chances that the senior will grant a favorable decision are slim. The informal meetings prior to the formal one will determine staff acceptance. In the formal meetings, the leader looks for or hopes for consensus. If there is any major objection at this meeting, prudent leaders generally will not force a decision. They often will table the issue and ask for more staff work. This is not the expected result for the person pushing the proposal.

The subordinate leader who can effectively work the staff can influence the agenda. Obtaining staff acceptance will help move the issue to decision. This is preferable to trying to obtain the decision as a surprise in a formal meeting.

One should remember, the staff's responsibility is to provide the senior leader with the best advice. All actions must go to the staff first. The staff must take a position and advise the leader. It is essential to get their support if a subordinate leader wishes to advance proposals.

THE ENEMY IS US

Napoleon said, "There are no bad regiments, only bad colonels." A student of organizational structure soon realizes that organizational problems lie in management, not in workers. Experience indicates that members of an organization will respond positively to the leadership and will work to please the senior leader (assuming that leader has not abused the individuals and made them enemies). So when organizations fail to accomplish their objectives, I believe it is simply a lack of effective leadership. Management is the problem, and managers need to become introspective and constantly ask what they are doing to hinder successful resolution of the problem. Once managers make that concession and earnestly look for the solution, the work force will help them and will develop new ways to successfully accomplish the mission.

On a trip to Israel in 1992, I visited an Israeli defense contractor who had a reputation for producing high-quality material. A contractor senior official commented to me that 99 percent of all quality problems are management's fault. Their position was: To improve quality, change management. I was impressed with the comment and started observing quality actions of the United States defense contractors. I concluded the Israeli statement is true. Good management does indeed improve the quality of the product.

NEVER GO OUT OF
YOUR WAY TO MAKE AN ENEMY

Never make an enemy needlessly. Many people, once promoted to a coveted job, feel they have been anointed and will always move to bigger and better heights. This is not true! Over the years, as I watched people move within an organization, I realized that successful people are nice to everyone on the way up. You never know what job the other person will have tomorrow.

I observed that at some time, every person will be passed over for promotion. This will occur for a variety of reasons. In the military, the generals and admirals have tremendous power and authority for the moment. Yet, they ultimately move on. The system is designed to move people up, through, and out. Even our elected President can serve only two terms. Industry is the same. Chief Executive Officers (CEOs) of large corporations stay on the job an average of 5 years. This being the case, power is fleeting, temporary, and in the end it is the individual who effectively interfaced with people that is successful. Making an enemy needlessly is wasted capital never to be regained.

Successful managers concentrate on the issues and leave personality conflicts behind.

Lawyers are a good example. They fight in court as advocates for a position, and then at a break, they have coffee together. Some people do not understand this type of behavior, but it is exactly this type of relationship that a leader needs to develop to work issues on another more amiable day. The person who makes an enemy will never obtain from that person a discretionary concession until a better personal relationship is developed. Interpersonal feelings will still be in the way.

MORAL COURAGE

One of the essential ingredients to effective leadership is moral courage. Individuals in leadership positions are often asked to make decisions and act in a manner inconsistent with their own personal desires or convictions. At DLA, I had the great pleasure to work with Raymond Chiesa. Chiesa was the senior procurement officer and a very competent manager. He supervised the expenditure of $11 billion a year and would often quote scripture to me when we were confronted with a tough decision neither of us wanted to make, but knew we had to. He often would say, "Let this cup pass from me." (Matthew 26:39, American Standard Bible)

Senior officials, particularly those who hold the public trust in government, must be mindful that they are called upon to make decisions that require moral courage. It is not enough to simply pick and choose. The job requires that you set the correct moral climate for the organization.

The procurement scandals of the late 1980s are strong examples. These scandals, termed "Operation Ill Wind" by the Justice Department, involved some senior corporate and government officials accepting illegal gratuities to obtain government contracts and gain an unfair advantage.

The leader must fundamentally know the difference between right and wrong. There can be no exceptions. To be an effective leader, you must have the courage to do what is right, regardless of the human tendency to go with the popular opinion or the easy way out.

In the fall of 1990, the department was working with progress payments for the C-17 aircraft program. The McDonnell Douglas Corporation was having a cash-flow problem, and its senior management appealed to DoD to increase the flow of progress payments. The arguments were lively and persuasive, and there was a strong feeling in government that the country needed to have McDonnell Douglas, as a corporation, survive and remain in the defense business. The argument also held that the government would be greatly harmed if the corporation went bankrupt. The primary issue, however, was how McDonnell Douglas had progressed with the work and how much in progress payments was due to the corporation. The question that required moral courage was how much money the company would receive. Some individuals argued that factors other than progress payments should be considered. Someone came up with the question of the company's urgency of need. Neither government procurement rules nor contract law recognizes urgency of need as a requirement to dispense government funds.

In such an instance, a large degree of Sunday-school values come in handy. The manager must know what is right, do what is right, and do it sometimes at great personal expense. Even though there is great pressure to "help cure" the problem, the one who has the authority must stand and decide what is right, not necessarily what others want done. Doing what is right will pay handsome dividends. That is what happened to the McDonnell Douglas C-17 progress payment request.

The defense official making the determination, Air Force Colonel Kenneth Tolleson, made the right decision. Disregarding the tremendous pressure by others more senior to him to find a way to dispense funds (that after the fact could not stand the hard test of a government audit), Tolleson held the line and said we will only dispense funds for what the contractor has performed to this point. (Tolleson and the contracting officer who worked for him were the only individuals vested with the authority to make that decision.) In so declaring, Tolleson greatly upset others, who were trying to find a way to ensure that the contractor did not run out of funds. As his immediate supervisor, I had advised Tolleson to do only what was "right."

After Tolleson's decision, I received calls from officials who suggested that maybe Tolleson was not the person for the job and should be removed. I responded, "Tell me where he is wrong according to law and regulation." They could not, for Tolleson, as I came to discover, was consistently correct. It takes a lot of courage to face the organizational seniors and go against their wishes. Tolleson in this case did just that, and in doing so he knew that any chance of being promoted to general was over as far us the Air Force was concerned.

General Norman Schwarzkopf, hero of the Gulf War, is quoted on the subject of character. "Leaders must have character, and non-character will do you in." Schwarzkopf is correct. Leadership is predominately a measure of character. Leaders are role models, both good and bad. Hitler was a great orator, but he had a bad character. Eisenhower was a role model and a true leader. Former Chief of Staff of the Army, General John Wickham, when asked, "Where are the Bradleys, the Pattons, and the MacArthurs of today?" would answer without hesitation, "They are there. We only need a war to bring them out." The Gulf War brought generals like Schwarzkopf, Pagonis, Yoesocks and others—true leaders who exhibited moral courage. It is the one ingredient that every successful leader has in addition to personal and professional integrity.

Another example of this quality occurred when I met John McDonnell, CEO of the McDonnell Douglas Corporation, to inform him that senior officials of the Defense Department were not pleased with his company's performance. He exhibited strong moral courage when he accepted the problem and moved to focus the senior leadership of the company on the issues and a series of action plans to get the company moving. The McDonnell Douglas Corporation is today a more efficient organization as a direct result of that demonstration of moral courage.

The footnote to this episode came in September 1993 when the Acting Department of Defense Inspector General Derek J. Vander Schaaf presented Tolleson a cash award of $10,000 for his actions. The ceremony was held in Washington, D.C., and I was invited and happy to be in the audience. Tolleson had many opportunities over the course of many months to be wrong. But his display of moral courage and his desire to do what was honest and right in the end was the factor that kept him on course. I would later use Tolleson as an example of outstanding moral courage. I would ask, "How many Ken Tollesons do I have in my command?" My goal was to have 100 percent.

CRITICAL MOMENTS

Every meeting has a critical time when the outcome will be determined. This time is often at the beginning of the meeting, but could occur at any point.

On a trip to Israel, I was to meet with the U.S. ambassador concerning contract administration of Israeli companies performing work on U.S. defense contracts. United States contracting officers were awarding contracts to Israeli contractors located in the Israel occupied zone. It was difficult and dangerous for our quality assurance specialists to travel to hostile territory to perform their duties. Something had to be done. I could not in good conscience send employees into an area where combatants were firing guns at innocent people on a daily basis. My staff had briefed me that the U.S. ambassador did not want to raise the issue with Washington about changing the policy, because he did not wish to "make waves." I wanted the U.S. government to place contractors located in hostile territory off limits to U.S. contracting authority and not award any contracts to them.

Going into the meeting with the ambassador, I felt we were placing my people at undue risk, and it didn't make any sense to me not to take the matter up with responsible people in Washington. I did not have a good feeling about the ambassador before the meeting started. From the start of the meeting, the ambassador was rather hostile toward me. It didn't take long for the subject of the U. S. contracting with firms operating in the occupied territory to come up. I braced to hear him dodge the issue. Instead, he asked me why I wanted U.S. contractors to keep making awards to these firms in the occupied zone since it put my people in danger when they traveled in the area. The ambassador said to me, very accusatorially, "Why do you want to continue this practice?" I replied, "Mr. Ambassador, I'm here to ask you to support eliminating the practice." He said, "I thought you were here to support the continuation." I told him I had been briefed that he was not about to make waves back in Washington. Tensions quickly cooled. He said, "Of course we shouldn't be placing American contracting specialists in jeopardy." We each won our point. The moral: In every meeting, both parties arrive with preconceived notions.

As a young lawyer, I once represented a husband in divorce court. Another lawyer had represented him, and the judge had issued an adverse decision against him. My client requested my assistance in reclaiming his Cadillac. As the couple split on their last evening together, the wife took the keys to my client's Cadillac and drove off, leaving her older Buick. Upon filing for divorce, she had his Cadillac in her possession, and he had her old Buick. I was able to get a new hearing before the judge on the subject of alimony and child support. At the hearing I was pleading for a reduction in alimony and child support. The judge almost threw me out of court on both issues. I was disheartened. I felt I had prepared a good case for a reduction in the money that my client would have to pay. The judge refused to change the amount. He said to me, "Is there anything else that you want?" I had almost forgotten that my original task was to obtain possession of my client's Cadillac. I said, "Yes, your honor. She's got his Cadillac. He's got her Buick. And we'd like to give her back her Buick and take his Cadillac." The judge looked at me, grinned, and said, "Well, you have won nothing else. So ordered. He can have the Cadillac." My client was ecstatic! He jumped up, hugged me, and said, "Hell, that's what I asked you to do for me to begin with." In his eyes I had won, in mine I felt that I had lost.

This event taught me the value of understanding and focusing upon what one is supposed to do. In this case, my client wanted his car back. That is why he came to me in the first place. While if I had been successful he would have been happy,

I had expanded my role. I also, until the last moment, had forgotten about my original purpose. This is an often fatal trait.

A leader, to be successful, should be focused and should not operate outside the framework of the original task. Also, the leader must be alert at critical decision points to be able to capture the moment and the advantage.

THE GREAT COMMUNICATOR

In politics, America has seen former President Ronald Reagan referred to as the "great communicator." He could take complicated issues and reduce them to simple terms. Every leader must seek this ability. It works in politics, and it works in organizational settings.

I first discovered this technique when I was a battalion commander at Fort Lee, Virginia. I commanded over 800 soldiers at any one time. As I noted earlier, these soldiers were young men and women, often away from home for the first time in their lives. There were many physical conflicts between them, and almost instantly there could be a large-scale fight. To anticipate and to ward off this possibility, I would personally meet with each soldier arriving into the organization. I did this as a group each week. I pitched the notion that nothing should get to a point that would require the soldiers to resort to fist fights or brawls. I also told them that if they did, they would be in trouble with Army authorities and could lose money and their personal time doing extra duty.

One night, I was attending a formal affair in white dinner jacket. An aide whispered to me that a company from another battalion was marching toward my 1st Battalion "Charlie Company." I immediately grabbed my hat, jumped in the car, and soon arrived in the company area. I told the "charge of quarters" to get everybody in the company to report to me in the day room (large area equivalent to a living room). I quickly told my battalion that a group of soldiers were coming to cause a disturbance, and that no one was to respond—that no one's manhood or womanhood was in question. We were not going to have a fight! As the group of rowdy soldiers approached, I stood at the door, identified myself, and said, "You fellows came for a fight. However, you will end up with more than what you came for. I have instructed the 'charge of quarters' to call the military police in five minutes. My advice, turn around and go back to your barracks. There is no fight for you here, and tomorrow you will not be in trouble if you leave quietly and now." The issue was defused. Not because I was crazy enough to go against a group of rowdy and half-drunk soldiers, but because effective communication accomplished it. Effective communication to the lowest level does wonderful things. If a leader tells the work force honestly what is to be expected, it is my experience that the work force will respond positively.

History is filled with statesmen telling people the truth and having them accept it. Roosevelt, Churchill, Truman, and Eisenhower are good examples of leaders who have used this technique effectively. I believe people accept news, even bad news when they believe that it is coming from a leader who is honest and forthright. Too often, leaders in organizations tend to put a lid on bad or adverse news. They do not tell the work force what is happening and tend to feel that the longer they can keep something under wraps, the better they will be able to work it. I believe the opposite is true. Whatever the leader has to do, even if it is bad medicine, goes down with honesty and truthful disclosure.

DON'T DRINK YOUR OWN BATH WATER

In both government and industry, the leader is often placed upon a pedestal and given homage. Corporate chief executive officers, generals, admirals, and elected officials all are granted this lofty treatment.

The longer a person stays in the power position, the more the person begins to feel this attention is personal and not positional. Often, after individuals leave power positions, they experience a rude surprise, especially those who felt their favorable treatment was personal and justified. Thus the statement, "Don't drink your own bath water."

In the military, generals are just lucky colonels. Certainly, generals were good colonels, but all good colonels do not become generals. Those few that do are indeed lucky. One senior U.S. Army general commented, "If we lost this year's crop of brigadier generals in a plane crash, there are 50 other colonels ready to become brigadiers and the Army would never miss a beat." It is important for lucky individuals selected to general/admiral and other high positions to believe this is true.

The leader who understands this will be an effective boss that subordinates will want to support. Effective leaders take job issues seriously, but never themselves.

DEVELOP GOOD EMPLOYEE RELATIONS

The day of the successful autocrat ended some time ago. The successful leader of today values the employee as an asset, a powerful resource. The employee who is asked to contribute ideas is more valuable to the organization than the employee who is told, "Do it because I'm boss and I said so." There is a fine line between coddling and participation; but once given the opportunity to contribute, an employee will become self-actualizing and will make a better contribution to the organizational goals. The leader/manager who works with employees to answer the question, "What is it that we expect the organization to do?," will move quickly toward the goal. Then, monitoring performance with measurable specifics, this leader will set the organization on a course of success. I have found that this prescription will motivate employees to work to achieve the goal. In the end, employees have taken ownership of the task, creating an action-oriented group geared toward success.

Dr. W. Edwards Deming, who was quoted earlier, says to organizational managers, "Drive out fear in the work force." If an organization is going to make substantive change, it must do so without causing concern for their jobs among the work force. This is principally accomplished within the management's middle layers. Unless one can obtain the support of middle-level supervisors, work will be stymied; and it will be impossible for the leader to accomplish anything of importance because of the supervisors' reluctance to support the effort. Driving out fear and assuring the work force that they are part of the team and have job security is basic to organizational progress. This does not mean that jobs are never eliminated; but it does mean that once the organizational structure is developed, those employees that are placed in positions in the new structure must have job security or the leader will fail to materially accomplish the goals.

ASK THE RIGHT QUESTIONS

Leaders should learn to ask the right questions. Often the staff will know the answer to the problem, but meetings are conducted in such a way that the answer to a problem will not necessarily emerge. Conducting a productive meeting is the leader's responsibility.

Often in organizations, meetings are scripted; and very senior people go through the motions of a meeting without getting anything done. Two or three briefers will recite carefully rehearsed speeches and present their conclusions. In the end, each briefer will say to the senior, "This concludes my briefing. Are there any questions?" The senior responds, and ultimately makes a decision. In large settings it is entirely possible that someone present has relevant information that should be voiced. Meeting protocol, however, is such that almost no one is going to raise a hand and say, "This is wrong. I know something that needs to be added." This is particularly true if that individual is a much lower-ranking employee. The senior should understand that this is often the case and develop an atmosphere of participation. Before a decision is made, the senior should encourage active and open discussion with all participants in the meeting, or there is no reason to have the people in the meeting in the first place. Employees become more valuable when they feel they can contribute by presenting information, and the senior's decisions will be better if all relevant facts are out in the open. It is the leader's responsibility to set the tone so that this can happen.

REORGANIZE WITH CARE

In more than 33 years of government service, I have noticed that individuals who are taking over as head of an organization have a tendency to reorganize. To be sure, reorganizing gives the leader a very warm feeling. It has all the appearance of making major progress. It gets everybody up and moving and the creative juices flowing. However, reorganizing often gives the illusion of progress when nothing is really accomplished. It also creates work force insecurity. In every reorganization effort the question is, "What was the profitable outcome of the reorganization?" Second lieutenants in the military often will show that they are in charge of an organization by realigning the desk so that those who come in know that there is a new person in charge. Some senior officers with greater organizational responsibilities will reorganize and divide organizations, but unless the fabric of the unit is designed to truly change, only the organizational diagrams and the reporting relationships will be changed. To have real change, there must be an overt action on the part of the organization itself to stop doing things that are unproductive. Reorganization for reorganization's sake is counterproductive.

WHAT GETS MEASURED, GETS DONE

It is true that what gets measured also gets done. In large organizations, this simple fact is often overlooked. While many meetings take place, they become social gatherings. Members sit around and talk about the issue, but make progress only when an accounting of the outcome is required. The leader should focus on the issue of measuring what the group is doing up front and early in the process. This simple technique has more to do with progress than possibly any single element.

In today's total quality management atmosphere (yes, it is a buzz word), companies doing business with DoD are accepting the principle of statistical process control. The emphasis is to measure what is to be accomplished. The result is that to implement statistical process control, managers have to start measuring the output. They have to know how bad they are versus how good they are.

Deansgate Manufacturing Company of New Orleans, Louisiana, had been a supplier of Brooks Brothers clothing, and for reasons of their own, they decided to also produce military clothing. Brigadier General Mike Pepe, my director of quality at the time, called me one day and said, "With all the problems we are having with clothing contractors, there is one contractor producing clothing with virtually no quality defects." He suggested that I visit the company. I agreed to go. By the time I got there, Deansgate Manufacturing Company had achieved such a high degree of success that I was pleased to present them with DLA's award for Quality Excellence.

When I arrived, Bernard Davidson, the owner, and other company officials met us and were delighted to have someone from Washington come to see them. They had even invited Congresswoman Lindy Boggs to attend the ceremony. I asked, "What was it that made such a difference in producing such high quality clothing?" The plant manager told me that our quality assurance specialist informed him one day of the quality yields that Deansgate was getting at various points in the manufacturing process. The plant manager asked her, "Where did you get the information?" She responded that it was his information, that she had just collected it at her computer terminal and organized it in a form to measure the output. Immediately, the general manager ordered a computer to be placed in his office. He duplicated her data, and he was then able to know where he had problems in the manufacturing process. The company became very successful using this technique.

Such was the case of Deansgate Manufacturing Company and, as I was to learn, several other defense contractors. However, those contractors who did not see that change was coming and that the Department of Defense was going to rely only on those who were more efficient failed either to win new contracts or had serious financial difficulties in completing their existing contracts. In the end, a large number of defense contractors were forced out of business because of inefficiency. Leaders are paid to recognize trends and see where their business is heading. To do this they must be able to measure what their business units are really accomplishing.

THE 30-PERCENT RULE

As the Army's competition advocate general looking for ways to improve buying practices, I came to understand the value of the 30-percent rule. Stated simply: In most business transactions the total cost can be reduced by 30 percent by increasing efficiency. I believe that, in most situations, 30 percent of the total cost of a product or service can be negotiated to the benefit of the buyer.

As I reported the results of the Army's competition effort to (then Secretary of the Army) John O. Marsh, I emphasized that, once competition was introduced into a procurement, the difference between what the taxpayer previously paid under sole source and the new competitive purchase was an average of 30 percent. Later, as the DoD senior procurement official supervising the purchase of $11 billion annually in food, fuel, clothing, and medical supplies, I observed the same phenomenal 30-percent difference based upon the initial offers and the final price. This occurred through putting discipline into the acquisition process. We required those selling to justify their costs as reasonable and allowed the competitors in the marketplace to help drive the costs down. Increased competition and measuring to reduce scrap and rework often produced a 30 percent price difference.

To illustrate, simply look at gasoline prices at the pump of a lone gasoline station at the beginning of the interstate highway as compared to the prices of each of four gasoline stations located on a busy street corner. That lone station has a corner on the market and can command high prices without regard to competition.

Therefore, it behooves buyers to use competitive forces to their advantage. Sellers should ensure that their organization is measuring output, lowering scrap and inefficiency in the manufacturing process, and not attempting to pass these inefficient costs on to the buyers.

This is not just a case of beating 30 percent more out of the seller (in government procurement the rules say that the contractor always makes the offer, and it is the government who accepts). When a negotiator and the producer of the item start paying attention to the relevant factors, both at the beginning and at the end, this attention will tend to drive down the total cost. To be totally successful, the process starts with identifying a requirement and ends with the item rolling off the contractors' assembly line. Eliminating waste—both in administration and manufacturing—creates "best value." The organization that pays attention to eliminating waste will find that it is more efficient and economical. My charge to the procurement specialists was to target the procurement objective and pay 30 percent less than what we paid last time. While one will not always meet this objective, the quest for it will make the process more efficient.

BE A MENTOR

Leaders need to encourage and help develop subordinates. Sometimes, however, a subordinate's success might intimidate the leader. Facing that possibility, insecure leaders will try to smother the enthusiasm, energy, and capabilities of juniors, often to their own detriment and that of the organization. Wise leaders recognize that subordinates who receive compliments or credit, also reflect well on them and advance the organization's agenda. The more the leader promotes the virtues of a subordinate, the greater the loyalty developed by the subordinate, and the greater the personal enhancement for the leader. Certainly, working to enhance subordinates benefits the organization. It facilitates meeting goals, since positive words to third parties about a leader's "lieutenants" causes these individuals to work hard accomplishing the leader's organizational objectives. Leaders should understand that the more emphasis they place on promoting the worth of subordinates and enhancing their capabilities and attributes, the greater the dividends to both.

The leader who never passes down responsibility to subordinates is insecure. A major element of leadership is developing subordinates to exercise their own leadership. Therefore, the leader should make time in a very busy schedule to listen to and mentor subordinates. Some of my most gratifying times were those I spent with subordinates in their personal development. Particularly satisfying is seeing those subordinates reach senior leadership positions, and sometimes reminding me of a way I conducted myself that made a positive impression upon them. In most cases, I had long ago forgotten the incident.

Leaders leave legacies, both good and bad. Most would hope to leave a lasting, favorable legacy. In my opinion, that can only be done by the leader who is willing to share credit and put the organization and its people first. Recognizing the quality of a subordinate's work, and working to position that subordinate in the eyes of the organization for future advancement is a must for the successful leader. Thus, being a mentor to subordinates is not only desirable, it is expected. In this mentoring, the leader should praise subordinates for good work and refrain from embarrassing them when their efforts fall short. An easy hand and a big heart will go a long way toward helping those that are coming behind to emulate the best that they have noticed in the leader.

However, there is a fine line between helping subordinates develop professionally and developing a personal "pet" that the leader seems to always be pushing for advancement. The leader must work hard to avoid any suggestion of pushing a favorite. Every subordinate who catches the leader's eye is worth one good push; but, if the subordinate is good, that is all it will take. Repeated attempts to move a favored subordinate up in the organization suggest to me the old southern expression of trying to "make a silk purse out of a sow's ear."

If pushing too hard is a mistake, and I believe it is, then the reverse is also a mistake. Leaders who do not respect and look for ways to enhance subordinates cannot expect maximum effort. Such a small leadership effort pays such a large dividend that it is truly amazing so many leaders overlook it.

PUBLIC AFFAIRS

Leaders of large organizations are called upon to represent the organization in the media. Some senior officers or executives dread the thought of public exposure and often make serious mistakes because of their lack of knowledge or their inability to properly handle the media. The Army's public affairs office offers a group of officers well versed in dealing with the media. This office developed a training program for senior leaders, intelligently designed to teach media savvy—how to address tough questions. The Army teaches three things: smile, energy, pause. The interviewee in a live television interview should smile often, but not as much as former President Jimmy Carter. He or she should project energy by leaning forward and answering questions directly while maintaining eye contact with the interviewer. (Ever watch a shifty-eyed person on television? It is hard to trust anyone whose eyes move to avoid contact. Television magnifies this.) Finally, the interviewee should pause to look thoughtful and intelligent. The real trick is not to pause at the wrong moment...this can make anyone look dumb.

Some leaders are simply incapable of responding well to the media, and all leaders should honestly assess whether they are effective in this area. If they are not, they should avoid exposure at all costs. However, when the media want a story, they want someone in authority, not the public affairs officer. The leader who does not have the capability to deal well with the media should consider sending another organizational leader. On a major story, the media will not tolerate the public affairs officer speaking for the organization. They want "sound-bites" from those who are responsible for the operation.

A leader, in the course of dealing with television interviews, should never give a taped interview if it can be avoided. At the end of the Gulf War, CBS's *60 Minutes* came to DLA to do a story. Their initial approach was to do a story about how the 400,000 soldiers were effectively supplied during the 1991 Gulf War with Iraq. When they arrived, the situation changed dramatically. Leslie Stahl was the interviewer; and the big question became, "How many vehicle tires did the United States government have in the warehouse?" *60 Minutes* went to the warehouses with their cameras and shot pictures of the tires. There were an enormous number of tires, but they represented only a 90-day supply. Stahl and the program producer kept hammering away, insinuating that there was too much in the warehouse, that the taxpayers were footing the bill for an oversupply. The *60 Minutes* crew put many hours into developing the story. I was not a participant, but I watched the conduct of the crew in preparing the interview. At one point Stahl stopped the proceedings, looked at her producer, and said, "Where's the story?" I found it interesting that after all the hours that had been put into this story, neither the person doing the interview nor the producer knew where it was going.

When *60 Minutes* came to the agency, they were asking many questions, looking for the story. The agency felt that here was a "good news" story. The U.S. military logistics effort had been able to sustain a war half way around the world, and the soldier on the line had been provided what was needed to win the war. *60 Minutes*, on the other hand, looked at it as a business decision that there were too many tires, the warehouses were too full, and there was gross mismanagement. Somewhere between these two extremes lies the truth. However, I don't believe that *60 Minutes* conducted the interview objectively.

When dealing with the media, you are not an equal. The media, with a taped interview, have the authority to cut and paste, rearrange, and change. They may place things out of context. The only way to level the field is through a live interview. At least in a live interview, the facts or the arrangement is not in question. (Remember, rarely, if ever, is the entire interview used, even live—the media stop at their pleasure.)

The biggest leadership question is the personal qualities and interpersonal capabilities of the interviewee. Is this person equal to the task? Time spent learning how to deal with the media is a must for any leader.

START THE STAFF ACTION

Before organizations develop staff papers for the decision-maker, someone takes a position that develops into action. The first person working the issue must address basic questions and consider small decisions such as right or left, red or blue? This person inevitably brings "pet rocks" to the situation, beginning with a personal philosophy about the issue. The military teaches the "staff-study approach" to problem solving. In the staff-study approach, you gather the facts, then make assumptions. Then you place the facts and the assumptions together, analyze them, and draw conclusions. From this, you make recommendations to the decision-maker.

I have found in government that individuals who initiate decision documents bring their own agenda to the issue. It is very difficult to have a Republican think like a Democrat, and vice versa. So, if you are looking for a Republican solution, you should not ask a Democrat. The same thing holds true in organizations. Often the problem is that the decision-maker does not know the agenda of the action officer. The decision-maker must constantly probe to make sure a decision is not based on questionable facts which, in effect, will lead to a bad decision.

Here is an example to illustrate how decisions can be made for wrong reasons. At the tail end of the Bush presidency, DoD officials wanted to create an additional joint service logistical command. The services were consolidating supply depots. They were fighting the issue of transferring and consolidating the logistics to DLA. (They were not so much against DLA, as protective of their own full measure of control.) To resolve the issue, a deputy assistant secretary of defense concluded that a new organization, called Joint Logistics Systems Center (JLSC), could be created instead of establishing the organization under the command structure of DLA.

The services liked the idea of a new command because they would trade one function and still have a part in another. The Air Force supported the creation and put a two-star general in charge, hoping to become the "executive agent" for logistical support for the Defense Department. All JLSC duties under DLA's charter should have been assigned to DLA. However, the decision-makers could not simply assign these functions to DLA because the services were still objecting to losing control. Therefore, they made a bad decision based on bad information. The footnote to this issue is that shortly after JLSC was formed, the Secretary of Defense remanded that decision and directed that the organization be assigned to DLA. Thus, what DLA could have initially added as additional requirements became a whole new command.

It is the leader's sole responsibility to stop and reflect; considering the facts and assumptions, does this course of action make sense? I call this a "sanity check" on decisions.

Because the "pet rocks" and personal interests of subordinates will have a bearing on the problem, the leader must ensure that "decision logic" can eliminate these factors and ensure that this decision is truly best for the organization.

A MEETING BETWEEN TWO ELEPHANTS

When there is a major difference between two organizations of equal status, staff officers of each will quickly work to establish their positions. A simple solution to the issue is impossible. I have found that one of the leader principals must call the other and suggest a nonthreatening meeting. This meeting must not be to argue the issues, but to establish a personal relationship so that issues can be resolved. When the two principal leaders have a cordial respect for each other, the problems created by the staffs become very small, and a solution can be found.

The reverse is also true. If the staffs have poisoned the minds of the leaders, it becomes impossible for the leaders to get together without showing the same disagreement that their staffs portray. Thus, no solutions can be found; and the problem must be moved higher up the chain.

Leaders are paid to find solutions. The capable leader will go to a meeting, understanding his staff's position but looking for opportunities to negotiate a win-win position with the leader on the other side.

THE ETHICAL PERSPECTIVE

In early 1990, various committees of the House Armed Services Committee conducted hearings about the ethical conduct of the Northrop Corporation in building the B-2 aircraft. It became very clear that ethics of defense contractors had taken on a new significance within Congress. The congressional committee had been especially critical of the Northrop Corporation and its past ethical practices. Some were advocating that the corporation be barred from doing business with the U.S. government.

John Betti, then defense under secretary for acquisition, asked me one day what we should do about Northrop's ethical "problem." I suggested we should contact the CEO, Kent Kresa, and see if he would be willing to work with us and frame a new approach to dealings between his company and the government. Betti agreed, and I called Kresa. Kresa was willing, and we agreed that the government would specify areas in which Northrop was deficient. Northrop would then examine those areas internally and establish its own action plan to correct the defects. Kresa would put a senior executive in charge of this program, and every 90 days corporate representatives and I would meet to assess progress.

The plan worked. Northrop's management tackled the problem with a great deal of energy. At every level we in the government started getting favorable reports about the changes they were making because of this action plan. In the end, I sent a government team in to check Northrop's ethics program, and the team reported to me that the corporation had successfully made the transition to emphasizing ethics in dealing with the U.S. government. I reported this favorable result to the under secretary of defense, and he accepted the report. Kresa led the corporation back to an acceptable level of ethics, and gradually those in government accepted Northrop's efforts as satisfactory. However, this progress was not made without a lot of skepticism on the part of many senior defense officials who felt Northrop could not change. Despite this skepticism, Betti was willing to take a chance for improvement and gave me the go-ahead. Fortunately the plan worked, and it saved a valuable contractor who performs a good service for the U.S. government and the American people.

Later, I attended a west coast meeting of defense contractors, and David C. Beard was speaking about Northrop's ethics program. He was the director of ethics in Northrop's B-2 division. Beard was articulate in presenting the Northrop ethical perspective. He observed that any decision that affects other people has ethical implications, and that every decision has an ethical dimension that can be evaluated in terms of adherence to ethical principles. He listed nine elements: honesty, integrity, promise-keeping, fairness, caring, respect for others, pursuit of excellence, loyalty, and accountability. Beard said that virtually all important decisions reflect the decision-maker's sensitivity and commitment to ethics. Hearing Beard, I felt good about what we had done and believed that Northrop had captured the management spirit of good ethics. Leadership cannot separate sensitivity and commitment to ethics from the overall goals of an organization.

CHEERLEADING

I do not believe that successful leaders can divorce themselves from motivating and inspiring subordinates. The organizational leader must keep people moving despite political, bureaucratic, and often complacent attitudes. The enthusiasm of the leader is contagious. Motivating and inspiring subordinates has a lasting effect, both on the subordinate and the leader. The leader who manages by sitting in an office reading and writing notes is missing a valuable opportunity. To be sure, not everyone will be as articulate as former President John Kennedy, but every leader should develop the ability to communicate. One should recognize that the political capital expended on communicating with employees pays handsome dividends.

In sports, as I will later discuss, coaches talk about the five-percent factor. The difference between winning and losing is often only five percent. To be sure, it is psychological; but once one gets momentum, it is hard to stop. This also happens in business.

It should be no surprise that the difference between a win and a loss is often small. The leader should program the organization to be the winner through personal enthusiasm and commitment to the project. The leader who is not committed to a project will have non-committed people working on the project. The leader who is committed and enthusiastic and grants authority and responsibility to the lowest level, all the while encouraging and inspiring the subordinates, will find the momentum that will put the organization in the winner's circle. You can not win every time, but you will not lose every one either. The key is to win more than you lose.

PART III

INDIVIDUAL
LEADERSHIP

....

Developing the Individual

I t is always easier to look down into an organization and see the things that people are doing to impress the boss than it is for those who aspire to promotion to look up and see the results of their actions. As a senior leader, particularly when I became a general officer, I began to notice trends. Employees are consistently enhancing or degrading their reputations. Here, I present my observations on people and their personal career development. These ideas are a mix of things one needs to do to advance, attitudes leaders need to assume, and actions leaders can take to help subordinates develop.

MEASURING ONE'S WORK

It seems relatively simple, but once workers start measuring their work through some degree of metrics, they are motivated to become more efficient by eliminating quality defects and improving individual productivity.

The Japanese auto makers realized this a few decades ago and established the quality circles concept. Quality circles allowed workers on the assembly line to meet periodically to talk about their work environment. They discussed what changes could be made to improve the process. A key element was that they measured this output so that they could know how much they improved. The process was very successful in Japan. The same principle applies to all workers. I have found that if workers are self-satisfied, have some control over their work environment, and feel they are contributing and that management listens to them, productivity increases. By measuring output, workers know when they are making progress.

In building DCMC, we noticed that as we gave more authority and responsibility to the quality assurance representatives, they took a more productive role in dealing with the company's management. On many occasions, company presidents would tell me how my quality assurance representatives contributed to improving the company's manufacturing process. Their work helped drive down unnecessary costs by improving the quality of the material delivered to the customer.

Companies started measuring their yields, my employees measured their output, and, in the end, productivity went up both for industry and for the government contract administration organization.

This message came back to me time and time again. I came to understand that one of the most important leadership tools is giving workers at the lowest organizational level authority and responsibility. The workers gain self-esteem, job satisfaction, and loyalty toward management. As a result, productivity increases in a climate where people pull together to accomplish for the common good.

WHEN IN TROUBLE, "FESS UP"

Professor Jerry Harvey of George Washington University, Washington, D.C., a management lecturer and consultant, tells an interesting management story. It seems a Japanese commercial airline pilot named "Osso" landed a plane in the San Francisco Bay, although everything was on schedule and the aircraft approach should have gone according to plan. Rescue squads recovered the passengers, and the usual question arose about how this happened. The media were in a frenzy. The inquiry started. Captain Osso was called to testify. People were expecting a long explanation about the malfunction of the equipment, bad weather, etc. In response to the question of why the plane landed in the San Francisco Bay, Captain Osso said simply, "I messed up." Those expecting a coverup were caught off guard. This explanation completely defused the tension, and the inquiry ended abruptly. While it is a humorous ending, there is a moral—when one makes a mistake, it is best to admit it.

In the hustle and bustle of business and organizational development, I believe everyone at some time or another will make a mistake of consequence. When this happens, you should immediately "fess up" to the boss. I feel the first to inform has a better chance to improve the outcome than one who "hunkers down" and waits for the inquiries to come.

In 1971, while serving as a logistics action officer in Vietnam, I was in charge of delivering U.S.-made armored tanks to the Republic of South Vietnam. One day, during conversation with a counterpart located in Sagami, Japan, we discovered a problem. My colleague said, "We're shipping these tanks to you in Vietnam. Our requirements are to put the radios and the radio wiring harnesses on the tanks with their antennas. If we put the antennas on the tanks, they are going to get broken." He said, "Why don't we drill and tap the holes in the tanks, then put the boxed antennas in the turret. When you get them in Vietnam, you can simply attach them and be operational." I thought that was a good idea and agreed. But I failed to get a copy of the message he wrote that indicated that I had agreed to making a major change to the tanks delivery method. When the tanks arrived in Vietnam, the wiring harnesses and antennas had been stolen. Needless to say, the U.S. leadership was excited about the foul-up.

I first heard about the problem at three o'clock on a Sunday afternoon. Our general, not known for patience, summoned the staff of 13 colonels and me, a major. Arguably, I was the only one that really knew the situation about the tanks. When we got in to see the general, he was in a high lather. He wanted to send a message to the commanding general of Japan, chewing him out for delivering the tanks in such a deplorable condition. If this message went, I knew the U.S. counterpart in Japan would say I had agreed to the change. I could see my army career in ruins. I then said to the general, "General, there is only one person around here that knows the whole story about this issue, and that person is me. I'm responsible for this, but I can fix it if you will give me 24 hours. If I can't get it fixed in 24 hours, then you ought to fire me." (Of course, I knew that he **would** fire me if it became known that I had caused the problem.) The general smiled at me, and said, "Major, anybody that's got that much gall...go ahead. You have the time." Prior to the meeting, in a panic I had called a friend with the U.S. Army, Vietnam, inquiring if he could get his hands on radio wiring harnesses and antennas. He said, "Promise them anything. We'll get it for you even if we have to take them out of American tanks."

Although it took almost two weeks to get the tanks fully operational, everybody forgot about the initial difficulty. The key point here is not about getting antennas, but that when something goes wrong, the best defense is to aggressively "own up" to one's part in the situation and start working to improve it.

The inclination in large organizations is to point fingers at an anonymous source. No one seems to know who is in charge. For example: Who is in change of and responsible for the United States monetary deficit? The President, present or past? Congress? Accountability is hard to assess.

The leader who accepts authority and responsibility (and the blame) will go a long way in building credentials within the organization. In fact, accepting responsibility and authority is an essential element of successful leadership.

SEND SHORT NOTES

One of the things that impresses me about successful people is that they have a tendency to send short notes, both to seniors and to subordinates. Generals and admirals are given special stationery imprinted with their number of stars for this purpose. I found the organization expects a senior to use this stationery. It is even taught to new generals at the "charm school." (When one goes from colonel to general, a school teaches them how to act like a general.)

It was Lieutenant General Don Babers who taught me the value of sending short notes. Upon my selection as brigadier general (but before I became one), Babers advised, "Chuck, you're going to get a lot of nice letters. Obtain some good stationery; and as these notes come in, write out thank-yous in longhand and return them quickly. It doesn't have to be long." He further said, "Don't put your notes on the word processor, and don't give it to the secretary. People will know it is canned. Take your time, and write each personally." What great advice!

I soon developed the habit of writing notes for all occasions. I kept a sufficient quantity of star stationery and envelopes with me at all times, and I would write "thank you" notes either late at night or first thing in the morning to those who had been hospitable to me. It is instantaneous. I've known some generals and admirals who wait three to four weeks to get a "thank you" note out on word processing. A lot of labor goes into such an organized effort. Someone drafts it, edits it, reviews it again, and finally the admiral or general himself will sign. This whole process has now taken much too long.

What is really required is a simple "thank you," for example: "Dear John, I want to thank you for taking your time and expending your effort to (have me over for dinner, pick me up at the airport, etc.)." A short "bread and butter" note is sufficient. We are not talking about a major epistle. The key is to say "thank you" and do it deliberately, quickly, and without a lot of fanfare.

All leaders should send personal notes, not just generals or admirals. Any leader can benefit from the practice. I once had a subordinate who was not a flag officer and was not given his own stationery, but he was a leader and had stationery printed with his name and address. Once he sent me a "thank you" note. I was impressed, and enjoyed receiving it. I have learned that seniors never tire of someone saying "thank you" to them. This is not "buttering up the boss." A genuine desire to say "thank you" shows class.

Business leaders often write a note to others on the back of a business card. This is probably not as effective as the note on stationery, but it is better than neglecting the "thank you" entirely. Leaders at all levels should communicate. A handwritten note in this electronic age is still a nice way to do it.

ENTHUSIASM

Many years ago I attended a seminar on marketing. The teacher made the case that "if you're going to be enthusiastic, you've got to act enthusiastic" and that anyone selling needs to be enthusiastic. Not many people buy from a salesperson who is down in the dumps.

There is a story about a life insurance salesman who approached a sales manager and said, "You don't want to buy any life insurance, do you?" With that the sales manager said, "No." The salesman said, "I thought not. Thank you." and started to leave. The sales manager looked up and said, "Come back in here, son. Look. You've done everything wrong as a salesman. I'm a sales manager. I teach others to sell. You should show enthusiasm. You should put your questions in the positive voice. Now, I will buy $100,000 worth of your life insurance." The salesman wrote the order, thanked the sales manager, and started to leave. The sales manager said, "Son, didn't they teach you how to sell in selling school?" To which the salesman said, "Yes sir, they did. This is the approach that I use on sales managers."

I cannot help notice the correlation between an effective salesperson and an effective leader. Professor Jerry Harvey of George Washington University has said that he has never met an effective leader who did not have a sense of humor. If enthusiasm is important and inspires confidence, then shouldn't all leaders develop some type of humor and enthusiasm and project these traits to the work force? I believe so.

The converse must also be true. The leader who is always "doom and gloom" with the world coming to an end is not going to inspire confidence, and the organization will take on these same traits.

The infectious enthusiasm of a leader—the laughter of Dwight Eisenhower, the humor of John Kennedy, the communication skills of Ronald Reagan—will go a long way toward making those in the organization feel good about what they are doing.

One day, I was having a discussion with a lieutenant colonel, who made an observation about another Army general. He said, "This general is always `gloom and doom.' Things are never good with him. Subordinates do not want to see these traits in their leaders, as they do not inspire confidence." A leader's job is to inspire confidence. Keep the energy level up.

Shortly after I was promoted to brigadier general, I worked a long day with a close associate of many years. I offhandedly made the comment, "Boy, I'm tired," to which she said very seriously, "Generals are never supposed to show that they are tired." Everybody knows that people get tired, but the leader has a unique relationship to the organization and, in effect, must not display this simple trait to the organization.

Enthusiasm is contagious, and people like to be around enthusiastic people. I have found this to be true, and enthusiasm can be a career multiplier. The choice between the laid back, lethargic, doom-and-gloom employee versus the enthusiastic, positive-approach employee is no contest, in my opinion.

I have found that no situation is ever so bad that you cannot display a positive attitude. I believe you should try to find the good in every situation and smile. If nothing else, co-workers start wondering what is going on, and that within itself can become a prescription for improvement. We are really speaking of energy. Energy is the force that will move others to greater productivity.

I once served with army Colonel Frank McCormick in Cleveland, Ohio, the finance officer for the organization. McCormick was a natural—always smiling and complimenting his subordinates about their productivity. It was quite something to see a finance officer get people charged up and energetic over bookkeeping entries, but McCormick could do it. He would call his people around him while he stood on a desk, and, with the zeal of a Baptist preacher, inspire them to great levels of productivity. He was a pleasure to observe. I knew he was special when I would meet his employees on the elevator, and they would tell me with pride how much they had accomplished toward their performance goals. To some, bookkeeping entries are dull business, but under McCormick's leadership employee energy abounded. McCormick himself was an bundle of energy. He was enthusiastic.

Taking a page from McCormick's book, while in Cleveland I often would get on the elevator on Monday mornings and, rather than turn around and face the door (as others did), I would allow the elevator door to close behind me, then say to a crowded elevator, "Okay. Heads up. It's Monday morning. Isn't it great? We have a whole week to give our best to our country." I would then give them my broadest smile. As soon as the door opened there was a stampede to get out of the elevator and away from this crazy man. But I did have fun watching their startled expressions.

Later in my career, I observed Air Force Colonel Robert Haines as one who could motivate employees with enthusiasm. When I met him, Haines was the personnel officer for DLA. He had been a fighter pilot in Vietnam. His enthusiasm was infectious. There was no problem he could not work out with his employees, and they had great confidence in him and his ability.

These two great officers taught me the value of enthusiasm and motivating employees with the same spirit. I came to understand that organizations led by enthusiastic leaders have enthusiastic employees. Things get done. It puts a period to the statement that if the leader is going to be enthusiastic, he or she must act enthusiastic.

To further illustrate, while serving in Vietnam toward the war's end, I visited my commanding general. He had been working long hours and looked tired and drawn. The North Vietnamese had, in March 1972, launched an offensive that was defeating the South Vietnamese. The Americans and the South Vietnamese leaders were very concerned. My job was to bring in supplies from the U.S. and give these supplies to the South Vietnamese Army. I briefed the general on my subject. The general looked at me and said, "Chuck, plan for 30 days and no more." As I left his office, I knew that the friendly forces were in deep trouble, but I also remember the feeling that I wished the general had been more reassuring. There are situations that do not call for enthusiasm, of course; but, from a leadership position, most things can be helped if the leader displays enthusiasm.

The successful leader keeps the energy level up by being positive and enthusiastic. A positive presence is required of every leader at any level.

CHARM SCHOOL

Once I was asked to speak about leadership to a group of newly promoted brigadiers. I have learned that there are some very common attributes the public expects a leader to have. One is culture. One must know which fork to use at the dinner table. A leader is also expected to be gracious. Leaders need to be able to say "thank you," genuinely and honestly.

In the Army, you must know what uniform to wear and make sure that it fits. The Army authorized a black sweater a few years ago, and it became so popular that people, in the absence of instructions to the contrary, wear it even when a coat and tie would be more appropriate. I joked to some, "The Army's idea of formal is black sweater and bow tie." It seems that at those occasions where it is obvious that a coat would be required, someone in the Army will always show up wearing the black sweater. It happened at my change of command in 1990 when we had many dignitaries, including ambassadors from foreign countries and the deputy under secretary of defense in attendance. Civilians expect military officers to dress appropriately for the occasion. There is a place for the military sweater, but it is not where most people are attired in coats and ties, particularly when members of other services are also in the service coat and tie.

Soon after I was promoted to brigadier, I was invited to the Association of United States Army's luncheon. I asked my staff what uniform to wear. I was told a short-sleeved shirt would be appropriate. I was the only person wearing short sleeves in a 300-person audience. Everyone else was in coat and tie. I was embarrassed and came to the conclusion that I could never be wrong wearing the military coat and the tie. I could always take the coat and the tie off. After that experience, I generally wore the uniform coat and found I was never in the wrong attire.

One footnote to the Army black sweater. Civilians do not normally approve of it. For the soldier it is comfortable, but certainly someone going before the media should not be wearing a sweater. Civilians, after watching military personal wearing sweaters on television, have remarked that the sweater does not look professional. It may be permissible, but one has to ask the question, "How is this going to look?" General George Patton said, "The farther up the flagpole you go, the more your [rear end] shows."

In the private sector, men are expected to wear coats. When an institution such as the military appears to favor an item such as the black sweater, they are expecting civilians to adjust their attitudes; this will not happen. There is more to be gained than lost in wearing the appropriate attire. Every discipline has a "dress code." The leader must be aware of this code and respond appropriately.

BOSS BASHING

In Sunday school, children are taught that if you are going to say something about someone, make it good. In organizational development, it seems that the national pastime is to sit around and grouse about the boss. Of course, there may be a legitimate reason for the complaint. If there is, most organizations have a formal procedure for making the boss aware of the grievance.

But that is not the issue here. What we are addressing is the idle griping that goes on in organizations without true specifics. One individual starts the complaint with gossip, and then others join in. In the end, a group of employees talk unspecifically about the boss. Invariably, the boss will find out about it. Remember, decisions on careers are based to a large degree on the senior's perception of the junior. Naturally, daily workday events create situations that bring on complaints. But, one should not engage in the indiscriminate complaining about the way the boss does or does not do things. At best, nothing will happen. At worst, it will work to the detriment of the employee. If conversation is not constructive to solving a problem, the employee should never engage in "boss bashing," for one derives no benefit at all from the exercise.

PERSISTENCE PAYS

If you want to do something enough or are looking for a favorable decision, the more you ask, the greater the chance of a favorable response. Persistence pays. However, if the organizational head has issued a final decision, you must go back to that person to have that decision changed. You must also know when the subject is closed. Efforts beyond that point will not be successful, and continued effort to obtain your favorable decision is counterproductive. It is in those cases where a final decision is pending, perhaps as the issue moves up the organization to subsequent decision-makers, that persistence pays.

I have found that, if a request is submitted on multiple occasions and in different forms, chances are that someone with authority will eventually approve it. One may need to refine the request, and it is best to have a reasonable request at the outset. Organizations tend to follow rules and regulations. The secret is to frame one's request so that it is within the organization's policies. The successful individual is the one who asks the question, "What will provide an incentive for a decision-maker to say `yes'?" Find the answer, then take your case to the decision-maker.

A few years ago, while practicing law, I handled a divorce case that another lawyer had taken before a judge and received a judgment. My client had $17 less than the total amount of his monthly income after subtracting debt payments, child support, and alimony from his monthly pay. This was unworkable, so he came to me and requested my help. I called the opposing attorney and suggested that he meet me at the judge's chambers to discuss the size of the award for alimony and child support. To my surprise, the opposing attorney showed up. (Since he had a judgment in his client's favor, he could have said "No," and I would have had no recourse.) The judge gave us a meeting. When we had presented our facts, the judge said, "If I did that, we ought to change it. I'll give you another hearing." Naturally, I was eager to accept, and we retried the case on its merits. Remember, if you ask enough people and are persistent enough, somebody in authority will ultimately approve your request.

Making a logical argument for a favorable response starts with persistence. First, gather all the facts, then align those facts with a logical argument, and present that argument to a decision-maker for resolution. It will pay off. You will not win all the time, but the percentages will be with you. You will win more than you lose.

Footnote: If the decision-maker has already decided the issue, do not go over that person's head for a decision. That behavior is disloyal to the decision-maker and to the organization. If an organizational issue has been decided and the boss has said to move out and execute, the employee only has two alternatives: do it or resign. It is only when the issue is **not final** that one can be persistent.

NEGOTIATIONS

The day that I was admitted to the Georgia state bar, I learned a very valuable lesson from the presiding judge. Before he admitted the new attorneys he said, "While you may be an advocate for a position, you are not an enemy with opposing counsel." He went on, "After you have fought in court and won, you should be the first person to the opponent counsel's table to offer congratulations in front of the client. Two things happen. You make opposing counsel look good, and you also make yourself look good in front of that counsel's client. Maybe the next time the client needs a lawyer, you will get the call."

Leaders in large organizations are often called on to negotiate issues. The tougher the issues, the more intense the negotiations. Borrowing from this wise judge, I found the same principle applies in day-to-day negotiations in organizational settings. When you make opponents look good before their bosses, it helps to negotiate your position. At times in negotiations, participants get emotional and the negotiations become personal. When personalities intrude into these negotiations, disaster results. When emotions are at stake, negotiating a reasonable solution becomes very difficult.

An example: Congress mandated that the military department ments create an Acquisition Corps and place responsible acquisition officers in the Corps so that the military services could be smarter and more efficient in purchasing. The Army allowed the personnel department to establish the basic rules for membership in the Acquisition Corps. As an end result, contracting officers who were charged with spending the taxpayer's money were excluded. But, by law, a contracting officer is the only person in the federal government who can spend a dollar of the taxpayer's money. A reasonable person would assume that if Congress mandates an Acquisition Corps, certainly it should include procurement officers. The personnel department in the Army did not think so.

As the senior uniformed procurement officer in the Army at the time, it fell on me to make the case to correct this decision. Congress helped, for it had passed additional legislation that supported the position of contracting officers in the Acquisition Corps. Negotiations between the various parties were very intense. Recalling the judge's wisdom, I dropped by to see the officer preparing the opposing position. I gave him a copy of our charts, and provided him all the data I had to make our case. (In law, this is called discovery—providing both sides with relevant information so that a judgment can be made based upon the merits of the case.) This tactic worked like magic. The officer accepted the charts and data, and later supported our position with the decision-maker. At the end of the meeting, I made an effort to say a good word to his boss about how professional he had been. Our relationship was always most cordial after that.

The key here is that one can advocate a position without being personally disagreeable. Never let business negotiations with those who hold opposing views become personal.

USE A PERSON'S NAME OFTEN

It has been said that the greatest sound in the English language is your own name coming from the lips of another. This is especially true when it comes from the lips of the senior

person in the organization. Imagine a presidential news conference, and the President of the United States calls a reporter by
name in front of a viewing audience of millions. It certainly en-
hances the individual reporter's status.

The same is true at any level in organizations. The leader
should get to know the people who are doing the work. In briefings, conferences, and meetings, the more the leader can use
the name of an individual, the greater the degree of self-esteem
from those who work for the organization. It may seem like a
small issue, but the technique works like magic.

I recall one instance when then Chairman of the Joint
Chiefs of Staff, General Colin Powell, referred to me by first
name in a staff meeting. It was a good, warm feeling. It does not
make any difference how high you go in the organization, the
sound of your name coming from the lips of a leader is a wonderful feeling.

To get maximum organizational and personal efficiency, the
leader should learn the names of organizational members and
use these names often.

VERBOSITY

People who work on complicated issues sometimes get the
feeling that everybody else wants to know all that they know
about a subject. Contrary to this perception, decision-makers
generally wish only to know, in clear, concise terms, why they
should decide on option A or option B.

An action officer preparing supporting data should be aware
that the environment changes when a proposal goes to the decision-maker. Generally, the decision-maker does not need, nor
want, all of the background; however, the action officer should
be sufficiently prepared to answer intricate questions on the
subject.

There are two different elements. Preparation will allow the
action officer to be competent, but additional preparation is required for the action officer to present to the decision-maker
only the necessary information in clear, concise terms. If this

takes only 30 seconds, use only 30 seconds, not 5 minutes. The action officer not fully prepared tends to approach the decision-maker and explain everything about the subject, thus forcing the decision-maker to pick and choose among the elements. This situation exemplifies incomplete staff work that will impress no one. But, the busy leader will value the staff officer who can take complicated issues, reduce them to simple terms, and present them in the briefest amount of time. I always valued the subordinate who, while allotted 30 minutes for a meeting with me, could provide meaningful information in an understandable format ready for a decision, and do it in less time.

KEEP IT SIMPLE

In a similar vein, I find that the more educated and informed people become, the greater the tendency to try to complicate issues. The leader who can reduce complex issues and thoughts into relatively simple terms will go a long way toward defining the agenda. To be successful, the leader must issue announcements, directives, and regulations to the organization in clear simple language. One cannot overemphasize this point. An organization whose leader's pronouncements are concise and simple will be much more capable of achieving its objectives.

THE ORGANIZATIONAL INVISIBLE WALL

Leaders have a lot of demands, both internal and external, upon their time. Some leaders build an invisible wall around them through their subordinates, and they operate within that wall. They accept what the subordinates give them and deny themselves the ability to assess the circumstances. These leaders cut themselves off from reality, and may operate within an artificial shell where the subordinates become the true decision-makers because of their influence. Leaders at all levels in government and industry are vulnerable, but this syndrome particularly affects the most senior leaders. A senior subordinate once said to me, "If you would let me, I would have you sitting in a corner within 60 days, and I would truly be in charge." This situation happens more often than leaders care to admit. The higher one goes in the hierarchy, the more this tendency can become a reality. Certainly, a President can become captive to the office. The news media labeled former President George Bush as such, and attributed his presidential defeat to being out of touch with the people.

Generals, admirals, and chief executive officers can also fall prey to isolation. A leader should explore ways to penetrate the "invisible wall." To avoid this pitfall, I developed a policy of accessibility, and the result was tremendous. Not only did it accommodate industry for whatever problems occurred, but it precluded my own organization from building the invisible wall. The staff knew that corporate executives often met with me. I did not require my staff to do the "pre-read" papers or determine agendas prior to our meeting. I was simply available, and if something came out of the meeting with industry requiring action, we would do it. Then I would respond to the corporate executive.

This seems relatively simple, but it eliminated the normal reaction of, "What do you want to see the general about? Please send a letter detailing your issue..." that normally occurs between two parties meeting for the first time. Subordinates will often do everything they can to keep the leader from meeting with outsiders informally. A leader who does not overcome the organizational propensity to require a lot of pre-meeting information from visitors can become isolated and inaccessible to important contacts. This is not the way to conduct business. The leader **must** be accessible to the outside interests of the organization.

HAVE EMPATHY FOR OTHER PEOPLE

A successful leader has, and can manifest, empathy for the problems of others. The most striking example of how one can live or die by this principle was that of a good friend who was running a large operation that was paying government contractors for their services. His organization changed the payment procedures so that timely payment to (industry) contractors for their services subsequently became a problem. This is nothing unusual in government. The issue here was the way the leader handled the situation. I know this individual to be as professionally competent as anyone that I have ever been associated with. He was a good general. However, the perception on Capitol Hill and in the congressional staff committees was that he personally was the problem. A senior staffer, speaking about my friend, said that he did not manifest sufficient concern for the financial plight of the small business community. What a damning indictment. This senior staffer went on to say that small businessmen were afraid to speak to the general because they felt he would retaliate and they would never get paid nor benefit from future business.

This did not describe the individual I had known and worked with for many years. However, I must admit that the evidence pointed toward affirming what the house staffer said. I believe the issue was that, while my friend felt personal concern, he did not manifest that concern. He had the ability to set the organization on a strong course that would have prevented this perception from occurring. It would certainly have prevented the necessity for a congressional hearing on the subject of non-payment to the small business community. He did not do any of this, however. In my opinion, if he had, it would have preserved a very fine career.

The congressional staff officer who was a principal in the hearings on the issue told me, "You know that I respect generals, but his unavailability to these people and his insensitivity to their problem was intolerable. He had to go. I'm sorry." In the end, the individual resigned and retired from the service.

Being accessible will not solve all of a leader's problems, but being inaccessible can be a career terminator. The lesson here is that the leader has to be the moral conscience. The leader must say, "Is this right? Are the actions of this organization and are my actions correct from a standpoint of `do unto others as you would have them do unto you?'" If an action does not pass that simple test, then the leader, who has the power to make the effective and immediate change in the organization, should do so.

DEMONSTRATE GOOD PHONE MANNERS

In government and corporate environments, leaders receive a large number of telephone calls daily. The leader should recognize the importance of returning each phone call promptly. As a junior officer, I made an attempt to return all phone calls in the same day. As I became more senior in rank, I found that returning all calls daily became very difficult. (Marketing telephone calls trying to sell you something, of course, need not be returned.) If I was unable to personally return a call during the day, I would have a staff member return the call for me. This did two things. First, if there was an urgency, we knew about it. And second, it indicated to callers that I was not being inaccessible, but was working my way back to them. I have found, that in telephone etiquette, a personal courtesy can prove very advantageous; and, conversely, a personal slight will always be remembered.

One of my "pet peeves" is a "holier than thou" attitude. Many executives feel their rank and their standing in an organization means that the person calling, or the junior in rank, should always be on the phone first. This practice is fostered to a large degree by the secretaries. The senior's secretary will often say to the junior's secretary, "Put your boss on the line—and I'll get mine." This practice consumes a lot of unnecessary time. My advice: make your own phone calls. Once, in calling another executive, I overheard the secretary say that I was calling and "was already on the line." For the busy executive this technique is a timesaver. A secondary benefit is befriending secretaries, and that alone is significant, for they can help you get your job done faster. The protocol of who gets on the phone first is really unimportant.

MAKE FRIENDS WITH SECRETARIES AND CLERKS

One of the most profound pieces of advice I received as a young lawyer was from the judge who admitted me to practice before the Georgia courts. His advice: "You lawyers may think that you are very smart, and you probably are intelligent or you wouldn't be here, but remember, your success will be in your ability to get things done. Make friends with secretaries and clerks. The secretaries and clerks will hold the key to your being able to perform your job." Boy, was he right!

I had a case involving child custody for which there was no written law. I had no text to advise me what to do. It was an issue that had to be resolved for the child's benefit. I called the clerk of the court and truthfully said, "I'm a new lawyer. This is one of my first cases. I've searched the law, and I cannot find an answer to this question. Can you help me?" Her response was heartening. She said, "Of course. I know how to do it, and the poor child. Come see me and I'll help you." I went to her as fast as I could, and she did help. I won the case for the benefit of the child. I was eternally grateful to this lady, and I had learned a very valuable lesson.

As I rose in rank in the Army, I always made it a point to stop and talk to the secretaries and the clerks in the senior government official's outer office. And, of course, I also made my own phone calls. I was always on the line when they answered the phone, and we could have a moment to chat. That interface paid handsome dividends to me over the years. It helps in breaking through the corporate veil, getting an appointment, and even getting the individual on the phone faster. If the secretaries want to help you, they will generally find a way to make it happen. One should remember that a good relationship with these important people is a must.

The converse is also true. If you feel that your importance so outweighs that of the clerks and secretaries, they will sense that attitude and respond in a similar manner.

HONEY VERSUS VINEGAR

In reorganizing, there are winners and losers. The leader should look for opportunities to make both the gaining organization and the losing organization winners. The natural tendency is for people in the gaining organization to conclude that the incoming organization is a mess, totally lacking in intelligence, direction, and leadership. Those in the losing organization will believe the gaining organization is oppressive, overbearing, and will be the cause of all problems past and present. While there may be elements of truth in each, the tendency is to speak ill of the other. The leader who gives specific guidance to eliminate this negative reaction and the ill will that accompanies it will be on the road to successfully consolidating the two organizations.

There is an old adage in organizations: If one is a member of a subordinate organization, the next higher headquarters is always wrong; the subordinate headquarters is always right. The reverse is true if one is a member of the higher unit. In this case the subordinate headquarters can do no good, and only divine wisdom comes from the higher headquarters. A leader should understand this organizational dynamic and should work toward eliminating verbalization of "the other guy is no good."

You can see how this works when you look at what happened when DoD directed that all pay functions for defense contractors be consolidated into one central agency—the Defense Finance and Accounting Agency. Previously, the pay function had been performed by DCMC. Paying defense contractors was a tremendous effort. In 1991, the average payment per work day to the defense industry was approximately $200 million. But, consolidating all pay functions into a central command was also a gargantuan effort. At consolidation, the tendency of these two organizations to speak ill of each other was preeminent.

Al Conti, the new chief of the gaining agency, and I met and agreed that each of us would concede 60 percent to every issue, and we relayed this to our respective organizations. My instruction to our contracting officers was that under no circumstances would they represent that we were no longer responsible for making payments to industry. The contracting officers could state the truth that the pay function had been transferred to another agency; but that as long as the contractor had not been paid, the contracting officer would still be responsible to work with the new paying agency to help facilitate payment to the contractor. To be sure, the contracting officer's job was not an easy task, but this approach did place responsibility on the losing organization; thus assuring a clean handoff to the gaining organization. In retrospect, I believe that this simple instruction was the most important element in establishing the proper climate to work the "pay issue."

By the same token, Conti told his organization that they could not plead that the old organization (my unit) did sloppy work or gave them incomplete files to absolve themselves of the responsibility to make timely payments. While I do not attempt to indicate that everything was good (in fact there were a lot of problems in making timely payment to industry), the new finance organization did set about to work positively to ensure that the files were correct and payment was made to the contractor. It certainly required a consolidated effort between the organizations.

This is an example of how the organization will respond when two leaders meet and agree on a course of action designed to reduce the "they done me wrong" attitude. Good leadership is anticipating what the organizational response will be to a particular situation and designing and implementing a positive course of action that will lead to success.

DEAL WITH WINNERS

As I progressed in rank, I noticed one thing: it was a lot easier to deal with winners than with losers. Winners are enthusiastic, have positive attitudes, are accomplished, and generally are more fun to work with. Winners generally do not engage in pettiness. Winners generally are not so personally insecure as to make those around them miserable.

There are two basic reasons to deal with winners. First, things get done more productively and effectively. During my active duty army service, I acquired some rental property. In dealing with renters, I quickly discovered that winners cost less money. The loser never seems to be able to put things together. There is always "woe is me," and it is always somebody else's fault why something does not get done on time or within cost.

The same principle applies in an organization. Some people cannot put together a proper plan and bring it to fruition. When one deals with this type person or an organization led by this type person, failure is the expected result unless an outside, extraordinary effort is exerted to influence the outcome.

The second reason to deal with winners is that being around winners is good for your career. Winners tend to help subordinates. Winners tend to place subordinates in an environment where they can grow and improve. A winner will understand a positive career move and will encourage subordinates to take advantage of it. Winners will never stand in a subordinate's path when a better job offer comes along. The winner recognizes that upward career movement is a natural order, and that winners enrich themselves when they help and encourage their subordinates to excel.

While, in government organizations, it is not always possible to pick your boss, it is often possible to "work the assignment" to be assigned to the "winner's" staff. In civilian organizations, I would say, "Never accept a job with a loser." If you later find that you have, then I would encourage that you seek a new job or reassignment.

LOYALTY

Loyalty is worth its weight in gold. The one issue that leaders generally discuss among themselves is the value of loyalty. Loyalty to the organization and loyalty to the leader are essential attributes an employee. Some employees engage in verbally belittling the boss to others. As I discussed earlier, this negative conversation will generally get back to the boss, and I have never seen a situation where it was productive to engage in "running the boss down." On the other hand, the loyal employee, the employee who goes out of the way to show a commitment is valued. I have heard senior leaders comment that if there is a question between going for the brilliant mind or going for loyalty, they take loyalty any day.

The question leaders often ask is, "Is this person a team player?" (It is important to know that we are not addressing illegal conduct. One should never participate in this activity. It is illegal. Period.) Leaders in the organization look for team players—people who can take the organization's objectives and make things happen without having the next senior leader constantly direct the effort.

I believe if you cannot work for your superior, you should resign or transfer to another organization. Leaders have every reason to expect employee loyalty and devotion to duty from their employees.

Rear Admiral Grover Chester Heffner, Supply Corps, United States Navy, a former commander of the Defense Construction Supply Center in Columbus, Ohio, tells this story: Navy supply corps admirals were meeting to select new admirals. Prior to the board meeting, the admirals were having coffee when an aide to the senior admiral walked in. The admiral had a pet project requiring a $10 contribution from individuals. Unrelated to the business at hand, the admiral asked the aide, "How is it coming on the special project?" The aide answered that most of the contributions had come in. The admiral pressed the aide for the names of individuals who had not contributed. The aide responded. Among the names was an officer whose record would be before the board for selection to admiral. Ultimately, this officer was not selected for advancement. The feeling was that if this individual could not support his boss on such a small request, then he was not the type to be an admiral in the United States Navy. I have found that at this level there is no shortage of good officers to be promoted to flag rank, and it is the seemingly insignificant detail that can foretell success of failure.

Loyalty is as close to a universally accepted concept among all leaders as you can get. If a leader feels that an employee is not loyal to either the organization or to the leader personally, there will be bad feelings toward the employee, and ultimately the situation will work to the employee's disadvantage.

Loyalty will not guarantee success; however, disloyalty will never be forgotten. The leader has every right to expect that the employees receiving pay for their services will be loyal to the organization and loyal to the organization's leadership. To be disloyal does irreparable harm to both the individual and to the organization. Leaders generally tolerate employees who make careless mistakes, but the one universal flaw that most leaders cannot tolerate in an employee is disloyalty. A disloyal employee may not be asked to resign; but once discovered, the relationship between the employee and the leader will be irreparably damaged. It is doubtful that the leader will ever express any confidence in the employee once the disloyalty is known.

While I mention illegalities and also present the option of resigning, I distinguish between two questions of ethics. The separate "blind" loyalty (my company right or wrong) from "true" loyalty. A truly loyal employee will call superiors to task on deviations from the organizations's objectives or principles, or from widely accepted ethical standards. It is my belief that there can be no margin of error in this area. As painful as it may be at times, true loyalty is the only choice.

THINK LIKE YOUR BOSS

Successful leaders are always ready to step into the next job when called upon. It is as though they had been preparing for that job, and it seems that the time limit between one job to the other is not necessarily a major factor. One does not have to have "a certain amount of time" in the old job to be appointed to the new. This is especially true of generals who move from the two- to three- and four-star rank. I recall that, in 1992, the Chairman of the Joint Chiefs of Staff, General John Shali-kashvili, was a three-star subordinate to General Colin Powell on the joint staff; and, within a year, he was promoted to four-star general and subsequently selected by the President of the United States to become the top military of-ficer in the nation.

So the question: "What is it that allows an individual to move from a lower position to a higher position and operate successfully?" It stands to reason that a subordinate's job is to make the boss look good. Every action a subordinate takes is de-signed for the betterment of the organization. The better the or-ganization performs, the better the superior will look. You cannot separate one from another. It is impossible to have a subordinate look good and a boss look bad (at least over the long run.) Employees who approach the job thinking like their boss, addressing the boss's needs, will succeed. An employee with the authority to implement a plan should, by all means, do so. If the action requires approval authority of the senior, then send it with a recommendation. The senior will appreciate having a subordinate who can think, plan, come to a conclusion, and present a workable recommendation. While not all such plans will be accepted, the employee will be viewed favorably; and when vacancies occur in the higher ranks, the employee will be a strong contender for the job.

SEX AND THE OFFICE

Probably no other subject can lead to more trouble in an or-ganization than overlooking or allowing sexual innuendoes among office staff members. This is particularly true when se-niors and subordinates are working together. It is especially in-appropriate if the leader engages in these practices. The early 1990s Tailhook episode of sexual harassment at the Las Vegas convention of Naval aviators puts a period to the sentence in the military environment—there shall not be sexual harassment in the workplace. However, while society is moving rapidly toward cultural change, I do not believe that training for managers has really made the point that one cannot nor should not engage in any type of sexual innuendo. Some will think a joke is funny, and they will think everyone enjoys it. In a business environment, sexual harassment degrades and, in the final analysis, is never productive. The reason sexual harassment is treated here in this very narrow scope is that it is a cancer that works against organizational productivity. The leader is responsible for everything that an organization does or fails to do. It is the leadership's responsibility to create a proper work climate. Sexual harassment at any level is never proper. A leader's primary job is to accomplish the mission and take care of the people. A leader who allows sexual harassment to become pervasive in the office is failing the major task of taking care of all the people.

Sexual harassment can take many forms, from small snide remarks to blatant proposals for sex. The issue is not one of degree, but of effective leadership that does not tolerate sexual impropriety.

As a battalion commander in 1978, I was the first commander at Fort Lee, Virginia, to allow women to be assigned to all elements of the battalion. Previously, women were allowed in the Army, but they had their own company and were set apart from the men. This practice was changing during the late 1970s, and women were being assigned to units where there were men. (However, the women lived on a different floor from the men.) Desert Shield and Desert Storm proved that this integration had been complete; but, this is not to say that there are not problems. Any time that sexually active men and women get together, there are going to be issues the leader must deal with. It is always the leader who must set the proper tone about this issue.

The public is intolerant of any type action that condones sexual harassment. The confirmation hearings for Supreme Court Justice Clarence Thomas and the allegations made by Anita Hill have placed a strong responsibility on the part of organizational leadership to ensure compliance. The leader must understand that the custom and the culture at some work places are moving along the line from some tolerance to no tolerance. A leader should not get caught with his policies on this subject out of "sync" with this fast-moving cultural change. It is best for the leader to communicate through appropriate instructions and through example that within the organization there will be no tolerance for any type of sexual misbehavior. As the courts render judgments in this area, the leader who does not take a proper and early stand on sexual misconduct and give the organization appropriate instructions could find personal liability for some future legal course of action.

SEEK HARD JOBS—AND GOOD BOSSES

Generals, admirals, and other leaders are often called upon to sit in judgment of others. This is particularly true in promoting military officers. Each military officer is given an efficiency report each year. Promotion boards look at the individual's entire record and make judgments as to whether the individual should be promoted to the next higher grade. In a military promotion the individual is not interviewed, only the file is reviewed. Having sat on a number of military promotion boards, I made observations about individual characteristics that help and hurt an individual. The first criterion, of course, is to perform your job in the best way possible. But, once persons mature in their professions to middle or upper management, it is hard to distinguish the difference between one person and another by the record. At this point, all performance reports are quite satisfactory. So the big question becomes, "What distinguishes one person from the other?" I believe the answer lies in the fact that the most successful individuals have sought out the hard jobs. These are people who took a personal risk. They took a "high visibility" job where if they failed, everyone knew.

I have also observed that successful people work for other successful people. The successful individual tends to take better care of employees. The last thing an individual should want is to work for an insecure supervisor. This individual is jealous of everything good that happens to a subordinate and will look for the opportunity to take credit for the employee's good work. The insecure leader generally tries to blame someone else when things go bad. The secure individual knows that organizations do things well when they give employees credit for outstanding performance.

Successful people are busy people. They are working for the organization, and they wish to see the organization grow and flourish. In my experience, successful leaders are not interested in taking credit for other people's work, whereas the insecure leader is.

Therefore, to have a satisfying career, you should seek the difficult jobs and look for the supervisor who has done the same and is successful and secure. Following this prescription, you will grow professionally and mature in the job, thus obtaining personal career fulfillment.

EMPLOYEE NEGOTIATIONS

Employees should know what is expected in the job. A prudent manager will ask employees what they expect to do in the near term and what they see as their total contribution to the organization. This effort will force the employee to become "goal oriented." Once the goal is established and the employee knows what is expected, the employee is "focused" and the organization is on a path to success. The leadership now measures the employee's progress by specifics. Employee ownership, acceptance, and understanding of the plan makes for a dynamic combination that is geared for success.

COMMUNICATE EFFECTIVELY

Leaders are asked to speak to the public and to address employees from time to time. A leader knows how to speak and write effectively. Granted, some may be better than others, but no leader can be truly successful who cannot inspire confidence in the employees or explain to the public why the organization is pursuing a certain course of action.

In the late 1960s, I served under Navy Rear Admiral Grover Chester Heffner at Columbus, Ohio, in a joint staff operation. Heffner was so insistent on the ability of his subordinates to speak and write effectively that he once asked an assistant, "How many of my military officers are members of Toastmasters (a club designed to improve one's ability at public speaking)?" The answer came back, "None." Heffner then directed all officers to join Toastmasters and have the meetings at lunch and on company time. I was a member of the group. The principles of public speaking that I learned in a few short weeks served me well over the rest of my military career. As a general officer, I found myself making more than 60 speeches a year to various groups. I believe anyone aspiring to a leadership role should spend time developing an ability to speak publicly.

Public speaking is not simply addressing a large audience; it can also include the briefings that action officers make to decision-makers. The leader can effectively apply principles learned in addressing large groups to these one-on-one sessions. All such opportunities help make the presenter a more effective communicator.

Writing effectively is equally important. Heffner also directed his officers to learn how to dictate. In character, he was very much like General George Patton of World War II fame. Very colorful. I remember his exact words, "I give you guys secretaries who can take dictation. If I find one of you writing out reports on a long yellow pad, I will fire you on the spot!" Needless to say, this got my attention. I learned to give dictation to a stenographer, and I must admit that this capability has been an essential tool in allowing me to do my job more effectively.

There is a correlation between dictation and effective public speaking. The key to all of this is to be able to reduce one's thoughts to concise statements and to project those thoughts to others in a manner that will produce a favorable reaction. Effective public speaking and writing are forms of art, but it is art that can be learned.

FOOLING SOME OF THE PEOPLE ALL THE TIME

Abraham Lincoln said, "You can fool some of the people all of the time, all of the people some of the time, but you can't fool all of the people all of the time." In a different vein, regardless of how good a leader is, and regardless of the merits of the case or how articulate that leader may be on a particular subject, it is impossible to convince 100 percent of the people all of the time, and maybe not even some of the time. This can be very disconcerting to the conscientious leader. In believing in a cause, the leader has a tendency to think that others should feel the same. This will not always happen. People approach different subjects from different viewpoints. This predetermined viewpoint will affect the outlook or acceptance of a proposal.

I became aware of this on a trip to Dallas, Texas. I was presenting a Defense Department plan called Exemplary Facilities to the defense industry. We were selling the concept that if defense contractors pay careful attention to the manufacturing process and measure output through statistical process control, productivity will improve. When this happens, the government can reduce the number of inspectors, and both the government and the contractor save money. We felt that the merits of the proposal were so strong that all in the defense industry would readily accept the plan. However, while I was somewhat successful, I was unable to convince 100 percent of the contractors that this plan was the greatest since "sliced bread." There were those who retained healthy skepticism for any program initiated by the government. Three years later, at this writing, debate on the merits of this proposal continues.

The lesson here is that a leader will not be able to convince all of the people all of the time. Concerned people will differ in opinion on the same subject. When you seek change, remember that you must approach the development of a plan with fairness and equable treatment for all concerned. You must adhere to the plan, always reassessing the fairness and equality issue. The goal should be a win-win solution. When one party loses on an issue, the winner has won only for the moment, and will again fight the loser on another front.

Former Army Chief of Staff General Gordon Sullivan says, "Success is adherence to the plan. He who executes fundamentals better than the next person will be more successful." A simple plan that is fair to all is a prescription for success.

KEEP YOUR MOUTH SHUT

It sometimes is hard for the successful leader to appreciate, but there are times to remain silent. Generals and admirals seem to suffer from always having their mouths open. Former Army Chief of Staff General John Wickham attributes this statement to General Omar Bradley: "When a general hangs up the uniform, he ought to hang up his mouth at the same time." I have been in many meetings where it was obvious that the senior, either from industry or government, though unaware of essential facts, felt compelled to impart "wisdom" to others. When someone who does not know insists on talking, that person's ignorance is readily apparent to all present. There are times when it is appropriate to keep the mouth shut. The key is to know when.

POWER DOES CORRUPT

As an old adage states: "Power corrupts. Absolute power corrupts absolutely." Most leaders learn early that the perks of the office and the position are fleeting and should not be considered a divine right to be held forever. To be sure, reasonable enjoyment of the perks is part of the rewards of being a leader. Problems arise, however, when pursuit of the perks becomes foremost. For example, note the military officer waiting for the soldier to salute him, rather than saluting the soldier first and saying, "Good morning, soldier." To be sure, the junior should always first salute the senior, but the senior who insists on absolute obedience misses the point.

Then there is the executive who is more concerned with the use of the corporate jet than the success of his business. In 1992, a CEO of a major corporation was fired. In the "golden parachute" negotiations, along with the large severance pay he was receiving, he requested the lifetime use of the corporate jet (which was denied). I have found that it is hard to work with individuals who are overly concerned with the perks of their positions. I believe you should take the job seriously, not yourself.

A leader cannot take advantage of the position. A very wise colonel once said to me, "Never insist on all the perks that come with the office. It is best to leave some." I came to respect that advice. In the case above, the individual was insensitive to how his official actions were perceived and was more concerned with perks. When he stepped over the line of propriety for something personal, his enemies were waiting. Perception is indeed reality. Enjoy the perks, but do not let the pursuit of the perks command how you approach the job.

EGO

All leaders have egos. Webster's dictionary defines ego as "the self, especially as contrasted with another self or the world." Some have larger egos than others, but one should never underestimate the ego of a superior.

In my military career, I served with many generals. I recall one respected general who possessed an even-tempered ego. He did not constantly need his ego fed by others, nor did he participate in ego-related issues. However, on one occasion a subordinate was being promoted to brigadier general. In normal military custom, the organization commander conducts the promotion ceremony of subordinates. In this case, the subordinate requested that another general outside the chain of command promote him. When the first general was invited to the promotion ceremony and found out that he was not conducting the promotion, his feelings were hurt. He went to the ceremony, but felt slighted. Quite possibly another more ego-prone general would have declined to attend.

During the Desert Shield/Desert Storm operation, I sent a respected colonel to Saudi Arabia. When he returned to the United States, a new general had assumed command of the colonel's parent organization. The colonel, rather than immediately paying a courtesy call on his immediate new boss, reported to his duty station in another state. It was two weeks before he went to see the general. The general noticed this small slight and did not like it. For the rest of the time these two were associated, the general did not consider the colonel a top-quality officer nor a contender for general officer. In conversations with me, the general went out of his way to be less than enthusiastic about the colonel's capabilities. I attributed these comments to the fact that the general was snubbed by the colonel at the outset. I came to understand that you should never underestimate the ego of a supervisor.

These are two instances where I observed that those who do not push the outer extreme of the ego-related issues can still have their feelings hurt by a seemingly small slight. The world has its share of those whose egos are so large that they get in the way—tyrants like Sadam Hussein who placed his picture on Iraqi money, or Adolph Hitler, whose ego was so large and projected such fear in others that his closest aides would not inform him of essential facts and events during the last stages of World War II. (To illustrate, the Axis forces were running low on gasoline to move their machines and tanks. Hitler's aides would not tell him that he did not have enough gasoline to conduct future war operations.) Unfortunately, one doesn't have to be a Hitler or a Hussein to have an ego. Most leaders do. However, good leaders have a healthy respect for their own egos, ensuring that they do not abuse the power that comes with the job.

THE GLASS HOUSE

Leaders live in glass houses. Therefore, they should be careful how they act both professionally and personally. You cannot ask employees to sacrifice through hardship, budget cuts, reductions in force, layoffs, etc. and then turn around and purchase big ticket items like expensive company cars, or a new set of china for the executive dining room, or take unnecessary trips with aides to vacation spots. When such actions are taken, you can be sure that someone will begin to question them. Leadership, by definition, places one in the limelight. Sometimes the leader is maligned with untruths; however, leaders will always have some people who wish them ill. These individuals are waiting for their opportunity to act. The leader's every action will be scrutinized.

Shortly after assuming the office of Vice President of the United States, Al Gore took on the task of streamlining the government. *The Washington Post* (March 1993) carried a story indicating that Gore was buying items for the vice presidential mansion that were unneeded and overly expensive. Chances are that Gore did not even know the nature of the expenditure nor was he a part of the decision. But, his enemies made their play. They charged Gore with misspending government money. The contractor doing the work was quoted "that the job was overspecified." Gore's enemies were claiming that he was being inconsistent: talking about improving the government, yet spending lavishly on his own living arrangements.

To further illustrate, take the case of a military officer whose hobby was repairing antique cars. He reported to a new job as commander of a large depot. Within short order, the employee union and he were at odds over many employee issues. At the same time, the commander had his antique cars parked in a government warehouse. There were allegations that he used government mechanics to work on his private car. (Whether or not he employed them never became an issue.) He was not the most liked leader, and with a strong union presence the employees wanted his dismissal. In the end, he was stripped of his command and forced into early retirement.

ATTENDING THE BOSS'S MEETINGS

On the surface, it seems obvious that attending the boss's meetings is important. Yet there are situations where individual subordinates feel that organizational rules do not apply to them.

I recall a meeting chaired by a senior general with subordinate admirals and generals. All individuals showed up on time Monday morning except one who came in late, apparently only because he found it inconvenient to travel on Sunday. This kind of reasoning is not prudent, for it sets up conflict with the boss. In such an incidence, the superior will probably not chastise, demote, or otherwise censor the individual; but be assured that the leader will mentally note the slight. In future actions, the subordinate must overcome the bad initial impression.

With the same senior officer, another junior officer would come to the conferences but never take his assigned seat. During the meetings, he was on the phone, dealing with other issues. Once the senior turned to me and said, "Why did he come to my conference if he is never here?" Seniors want subordinates to participate and be part of the meeting. Most importantly, it is not prudent for subordinates to suggest by their actions that other issues demand more attention than the superior's meeting.

There is an allegiance that the subordinate owes to the organization and to the superior. Subordinates should be mindful that they do not send the wrong message.

SPENDING YOUR SUBORDINATE'S MONEY

In 1959 as a new lieutenant, I learned a very valuable management principle from Army Colonel Austin A. Miller. Miller was my first army supervisor. My wife, Sandy, had just given birth to our daughter Kathryn. On a brand new second lieutenant's pay, our finances were tight. In those cases where subordinates were asked to financially contribute to a social event, Miller had a habit of calling the most junior officer in and asking inoffensively if he or she could afford the cost of the function. Years later I became very impressed with that technique. Not only does it help the junior in allowing him to support his boss's functions financially, but it goes to the very heart of leadership—taking care of the people. Austin Miller was indeed a remarkable man, and I was learning a valuable management technique from him.

In one particular event, another more senior colonel wanted all the post officers to attend his Christmas party at a cost of $40 per couple—a lot of money in 1959 since the base pay of a second lieutenant was $222.30 a month. Miller, who worked for the senior officer, very defiantly told him, "You can direct me to be there, and I will, but I have officers with small children, and with Christmas approaching, they cannot afford this expense. My officers will not be required to attend." Then Miller told us that the decision was completely ours to make with no pressure to attend. (It is hard to believe, but in the Army in 1959, junior officers did not have the luxury of saying, "No," to such events. They were expected to be there.) What an impression Miller made upon me. He was a great, caring leader—the first I had ever met. My devotion to Miller as a soldier was such that I would have followed him to hell and back.

At the opposite extreme, a few years ago I was invited to a General Officer's Conference in Texas to work military clothing and textiles issues. The host was a general who served in San Antonio where we were meeting. Most participants were from out of town and on expense accounts, but the invitations to the evening meal went to some local officers who were not on an expense account. A lieutenant colonel and his wife ordered frugally from the menu. There were 30 people in the group, and at the end of the evening the host general told an aide to simply divide the bill by the number of people and get each person's share. This takes care of the bill, of course, but for those on a limited budget, there is no way to control expenses. The junior officer and his wife were caught by surprise, for their share was more than they had ordered. They did not bring sufficient cash and were required to write a check. I am sure that they did not anticipate this large expense when accepting the invitation to attend.

This is not an isolated example; junior officers often find themselves in a situation they cannot control. The better position for the senior to take is to ensure that the organizers structure the evening's social event so that the maximum expense does not exceed the financial capabilities of the most junior officer present. This requires effort on the part of the senior officer, who will often have to scale back what the organizers have proposed. Organizers will want to go "first class," especially with senior leaders present. This is all the more reason for the senior to review the evening's plans ahead of time, lest the expense get out of control and unaffordable. The junior will appreciate this action by the senior. Seniors build their reputation that either they are concerned about subordinates, or they are not. Austin Miller taught me that at the very heart of leadership is a fundamental concern for the welfare of subordinates.

EMPLOYMENT RECOMMENDATIONS

A leader should be cautious when receiving a personal recommendation on a prospective employee from a previous supervisor. Unless the individual left under terrible conditions, supervisors find it very difficult to give anything but a good job recommendation. However, the individual's last two employers can often give a good characterization of the employee's work habits. It is not that the leader cannot trust the person's immediate supervisor, the issue is how to best evaluate the candidates applying for the job. It has been my experience that a little time between the person employed and the employer will often result in a more complete evaluation. The leaders must weigh these comments in light of the whole issue and make the best decision, recognizing that employment decisions are generally for long periods of time. Extremely competent people tend to move up the ladder rather rapidly; a person who is ill-suited to the organization tends to stay. The caution to the leader—do your homework to always hire the best person.

In employing people, be aware that personnel evaluation reports contain certain hidden codes. I recall one incident when the Air Force recommended an officer to me for employment. All indications were that the individual was technically competent and knowledgable about the subject matter. However, there was also a personal reference to his "directness." The hidden meaning was that this officer could not get along with others. To me this is a fatal flaw. You should seek people who are not only technically competent, but amiable with fellow employees in and out of the organization.

Dr. Jay R. Sculley, former assistant secretary of the Army for research, development, and acquisition, commented that his number-one requirement for employing someone is that he must like the person. Sometimes, I think that employers get caught up with the perception of competence and college degrees and forget that the individual must be able to get along with others in a day-to-day relationship, otherwise nothing gets done because of interpersonal conflicts. Employers should spend some time before hiring an individual to determine if the person will fit into the organization. If the answer is "no," then employ someone else.

LICKING YOUR WOUNDS

Every leader will suffer losses and setbacks. And sometimes the organization will fail to realize the desired objective or goal. A Georgia lawyer once said to me, "Take your loss and your disappointment, allow no more than two days to lick your wounds, and then get on with it." This is sage advice. When disappointment comes, allot a certain amount of time to feel bad, and then focus on the next goal and objective to achieve the next plateau.

When things are not going well, look for the good in the situation. Often, there is a hidden opportunity. One should treat adversity as an opportunity, for often success is just a matter of seeing an opportunity in what, at first blush, is a serious setback.

DOOM AND GLOOM

Some people are so intense that they appear to always have a personal problem. In relating to your superior, it is advisable to have some time for light-hearted conversation. Notwithstanding, you should endeavor to develop a positive attitude; if this is impossible, at least manifest a positive attitude some of the time. As an employer, it is hard to have a warm feeling about people who always respond, "Terrible," when asked how they are. This attitude denotes a negative reaction that both must overcome to move to issues that can be worked productively. If an employee always approaches the superior with a problem, the superior will reason that the employee has problems that he or she must solve or, at a minimum, must consistently cheer the employee out of the "doom and gloom" attitude. To be successful, you should simply tell the superior about a success—anything that does not require positive corrective action on the superior's part. The last thing you want to do is give the superior the impression that every contact with you is going to be a downer and a negative. Not all situations will be positive, to be sure, but you should not be negative as a matter of habit. Balance in attitude is the goal.

PROPER LANGUAGE IS ALWAYS APPROPRIATE

Some people feel that off-color jokes and language are appropriate. General George Patton's reputation was centered around his colorful language. Some have tried to emulate that type of behavior. I too have used it on occasion, but I have found that as America moves toward the 21st century, with a new emphasis on traditional mores and values, one should use language appropriate in any and all circumstances. In today's pluralistic work environment, people are not segmented by race, color, creed, sex, or national origin. A joke that makes fun of or is directly pointed to a particular group will definitely offend a member of that group and possibly others. Leaders of diverse organizations can ill afford to squander good capital in a manner that will pay nothing in return. While a joke may be funny, it is short-lived. The expense will be more costly to the individual than the use of the off-color joke. Since a leader has nothing to gain by using inappropriate language, always refrain from this type of activity.

A LEOPARD DOES NOT CHANGE HIS SPOTS

There is an old adage, "A leopard does not change his spots." The same can be said about people and their work habits. Having served on military promotion boards, I have noticed that individuals have certain traits that are so ingrained that to change them requires a "significant emotional event."

Having had the opportunity to judge people and make decisions concerning who will be promoted or selected in reductions in force, I easily concluded that it generally is not what is good about you but it is what is wrong with you that counts. Government particularly uses annual performance appraisals to make these selections. Human nature being what it is, unless the person is totally out of step with the organization, the immediate supervisor will not write a report that is damaging on its face. Organizationally, people become very adept at saying nice things about people while sending the message that something else is wrong. An example is when the supervisor says "a very honest and direct person" or "this person always tells it like it is," that is generally understood to mean "this person is inflexible." Interestingly, under a series of different supervisors, annual reports written on an employee will start highlighting certain traits—either good or bad. While an employee's supervisors over the years generally will not say "this employee should not be promoted," there will be signals supervisors will send about this individual.

My advice to the junior executive who aspires to senior leadership: Now is the time to develop your personal life and ethics so that when you are ready to assume a senior position, your character and the personal experiences in your life will meet the organizational morality test. With this foundation, you will not suffer from indiscretions that as a junior employee may not be considered important, but which as an aspiring senior executive become very important. A junior employee who is direct, sometimes rude, does not get along with others, and is uncompromising will have the same character as a senior employee. The employee who is motivated toward some type of sexual harassment—making off-color jokes or imposing unwarranted attention to the opposite sex—will, in all probability, continue to display the same characteristics.

Once I received a report that a senior colonel on my staff was having a sexual relationship with one of his subordinates. My first reaction was to disbelieve and give him the benefit of the doubt. However, I had to check out the allegations, if only to ensure that top management was not "sweeping serious personal defects under the rug." During the investigation, it became apparent that there was indeed something going on between this officer and a subordinate. The fact that he was having an adulterous relationship was singularly bad. But the fact that he was having this relationship with a subordinate was especially bad because it was having a very negative effect on office morale. (In cases like this, everybody in the office seems to know. The superior is the last to find out.) The conclusion was that he was favoring her with promotions to the detriment of the other employees; a fact that later was substantiated.

In this case, I called the colonel in and gave him the opportunity to resign, receive a letter of reprimand, or face charges in a court-martial trial. All the options were personally distasteful, for the colonel and I had been close business associates. It was at this point in the incident that I reviewed his entire personnel file. I also talked to associates who had known him for over 25 years. They were not surprised at his behavior. Those who knew him told me that he had previously exhibited a tendency toward this exact type of behavior and had been in trouble on the same subject before.

There are two management lessons here. First, a person generally does not change personal habits. Second, always check a person's previous work record before hiring. If there is a skeleton in the closet, generally the percentages favor the employee repeating such actions, unless the employee has confronted the issue and made a conscious change in habit. It is then up to the employer to determine whether the change is real or illusory.

COURTESIES

Politeness and personal consideration are hallmarks of our culture. The leader should never miss an opportunity to be gracious. Little things, like remembering names and birthdays, are very important. If an employee gets a, "Hey, you" from the leader, it is impersonal and the employee responds with little loyalty. As discussed earlier, using an individual's name, however, shows that the employee is important enough to have an identity. A good leader can capitalize on this. Leaders who are truly magnificent have mastered the names of junior employees. In business or social settings, they are able to call employees by their first names. A leader will realize immediate, positive results from addressing subordinates personally and inviting or asking their opinion on issues. This builds loyalty, confidence, devotion, and energy; and the employee will develop an allegiance to the individual leader.

Likewise, all people, regardless of their stations in an organization, enjoy personal recognition of their actions or positive traits. In speaking to the former Secretary of the Army, Michael Stone, I once complimented him. His comment was that compliments are nice to hear, regardless at what level you are in the organization.

The savvy leader will send birthday notes to employees. Obviously, when one is the head of a large organization, it may be impossible to send these notes to everyone, but the leader should send notes to those people who are closest as a small way of saying, "You are important, and I appreciate you." It shows concern. There is no other way to expend so little capital and get so much in return as proffering the small item of graciousness.

Therefore, regardless of what positions we have held, we really do not move too far from the lessons of the first grade: be sharing, nice, considerate, and polite. The leader who displays these traits will find the organization responding appropriately.

MAKE PEACE QUICKLY

In interpersonal communications people often have disagreements, either major or minor. But one thing is certain, every disagreement creates a relationship that eventually will need to be repaired.

Marriage counselors advise married couples, "Never go to bed angry." The same can be said of professional disagreements. This is particularly true when there has been a close personal relationship between the two parties. Generally, the friction created has come about because of a misunderstanding.

To illustrate how friendships and business arrangements can become entangled to a determent, consider the case of a senior major general and a colonel. The general was the colonel's mentor. The families were personally close. The colonel was promoted to brigadier general, largely because of the senior's help. A few years later, the junior officer was a house guest in the major general's home. A misunderstanding ensued over the sale of the junior's house. The major general's wife was the realtor, and the house was not selling. The junior officer, without talking to the realtor wife, changed the real estate listing to another agency. The whole thing came to a head at the dinner table in the senior's house when the junior revealed he had moved the listing to another agency. Needless to say, the conversation was very strained. Friends for many years, both felt that the other was wrong. The senior's feelings were hurt, and the relationship was permanently damaged. To my knowledge, neither has spoken to the other since.

Problems will always occur with interpersonal relationships. The smart individual will work to rapidly repair the damage resulting from a negative event—not necessarily for the immediate future—but for the long term. This fence mending is important, not only personally, but professionally. Often, organizations take on the character of individuals, and if an organization's leader has a misunderstanding with the leader of another organization, the two organizations will soon fight with each other. (It is easy to see how nations go to war!)

The advice: Make peace **quickly**. There will be other projects that each will wish to collaborate on—another day.

SELF-WORTH

Employees need to feel appreciated by the leader. Some leaders take the attitude that all they need to do is correct performance that is not up to their standards. This is very short sighted! Smart leaders will spend time complimenting employees and look for reasons to do so. One compliment in front of the organization regarding an individual's performance will have a great impact on the employee as well as the organization. Others will be encouraged to perform well so that the leader will do the same for them.

As a young Army officer, I recall working for a well-respected senior civil servant. He had a tendency to never say good things about an employee's performance. In a meeting one day, he said, "As long as you are performing okay, I will never say anything to you. I will only correct if I need to." I told him that it seemed to me that he would do a lot better if he would tell me when I was doing well, and when I didn't hear it I would know I needed to correct. The absence of recognition is more powerful than negative correction.

Years later, a subordinate senior employee approached me to talk about her performance appraisal. I had written that she was competent and capable. She, however, did not think my appraisal of her was as good as the last appraisal that she had received from me. I had failed to do my job with this trusted employee. In the hustle and bustle of working major issues, I had failed to spend that few minutes to compliment her, which was certainly in order, and to convey to her my impression that she was doing an excellent job.

I also want to mention the morale busting that occurs when some leaders feel insecure or threatened by a subordinate who is doing an exemplary job and take pains to slight or otherwise slam that employee whenever possible, and in the subtlest of terms. The real success of a leader is to see subordinates succeed. Not only does the subordinate grow, but the leader gains stature by the association. However, it does take a leader who is personally secure to recognize this fact. A moment spent telling an employee how important he or she is to the organization will pay handsome dividends to all.

FACE-TO-FACE MEETINGS

I learned the value of face-to-face meetings late in my career. Young professionals often become so concerned with learning the scope of their jobs and the technicalities of their functions, that they forget there are significant advantages to developing social relationships. One should never underestimate the value of a face-to-face meeting. Sometimes it pays to stop by to say, "Hello," even if nothing is on your mind. The same is true with phone calls. Telephone another to say, "Just thinking about you, and thought I would call and ask how are you doing." These brief encounters are great social capital. Like many people, as you work through your career, you may move from duty to duty or job to job. But, when you establish a social relationship, you will always be able to enjoy its rewards regardless of the position either of you find yourselves in at a later date. Maintaining personal contacts goes a long way in removing barriers to getting the job done.

ETHICS

Ethics is a personal code of honor that you either have or you don't have. To truly be a professional, you must have integrity and establish ethical values at the forefront, thus building a platform from which to operate. The pressures of wanting to succeed will sometimes become so intense that if you do not truly know yourself and have established ethical values, you may find yourself approaching the edge. This could lead to crossing that line into unethical behavior.

Issues are a throwaway. In the long run, when you look back over a period, a career, it is not so much the issues that were won, negotiated, or lost, but it was the principles by which you lived. A leader who will lay a principle on the negotiating table is a leader who will ultimately get into trouble. DoD procurement scandals of the past are good examples. One who negotiates away honesty or principles will ultimately lose. If you negotiate an issue and you lose, it will not affect your reputation or ability to negotiate again tomorrow. If you lay a principle on the table and you lose that principle, you lose everything. It goes to character. It is an expensive lesson for some, and no leader can afford the gamble.

This does not happen suddenly; an individual who professionally excels and achieves a high career position either in government or industry does not really set out to "screw up by the numbers." I do not believe that a senior appointed official or a senior corporate executive wakes up one morning and says, "I believe that I'm going to go out and commit a felony. This is the day that I am going to really ruin my reputation." I believe what happens is that people fail to recognize the importance of establishing a clear personal code of integrity. All individuals should know the line that they cannot cross. I believe that once you establish this point, you will be free to operate, knowing on which side of the ethical line you stand. However, if you do not establish clear moral values for yourself, then you risk crossing the line and finding yourself in serious trouble.

There comes a time in leadership when the leader has to say "Stop" or "Start." The leader cannot take a passive role. In the recent Navy Tailhook scandal, where the naval aviators conducted a Las Vegas convention that has been characterized as a drunken brawl focusing upon unwarranted sexual attention, the major issue centered around leadership. A naval aviator who worked for me during that time did not attend the Tailhook convention and had not for many years. In response to my asking why not, he said to me that he knew that the convention was a brawl and that the Navy leadership also knew about the propensity for it to get rough. He did not want to be a part of it. In preparing for the convention, the organizers would set aside a breakage fund to compensate for damage. This type convention had been going on for many years.

A leader cannot be passive when there has been a cultural change or when an organization is doing things that cannot be tolerated. In my opinion, what happened in Tailhook is that attitudes and behavior had been the same for many years. The culture and the sexual attitudes towards females, however, changed rapidly. Thus, the leadership was held accountable. This is as it should be, for a leader is responsible for everything an organization does or fails to do.

The question is, however, from a leadership standpoint, what does one do? The final conclusion is that a leader can never be "off guard" ethically. The leader has to have his "finger on the pulse" of the organizational culture. If suspect actions are taking place, the leadership should constantly assess these actions. Are they legal, moral, and defensible now or in the future if called into question? If the answer to these questions is ever negative, the leader must take quick, positive corrective action. Otherwise, that leader will be held accountable, and rightly so.

Getting to the heart of this, subordinates look for honesty in leadership. The leader who projects dishonesty has no credibility and cannot lead effectively, since the subordinates do not have a level of trust.

One of the greatest compliments I received was from an employee in Atlanta after we had reorganized and reduced the organization's staffing by 4,000 people. On my last trip to Atlanta before retiring, an employee said, "I want to thank you because you were honest with us. We did not know whether to believe you initially or not, but we knew you (I had served in Atlanta as a junior officer) and we trusted you." Now I do not say this as an example of my greatness, but to point out that honesty has to rank high on the list of the leader's attributes. Remember that, although you can be a leader in title by virtue of the position, you must earn the respect of employees through actions.

ANSWERING THE QUESTION

Too often, in attempting to sell a program, people forget the basic fundamentals of selling: opening, discussing, and closing. The opening is to introduce the idea or concept, discussing is to describe, and closing is to sell the idea and get the other party to "buy." In the stress of making a presentation, juniors often will not be able to respond to a senior's question. They often say something like, "I'm coming to that," or, "Wait." The seller should be able to field the question, respond briefly, and return, if necessary, to the presentation.

In merchandising classes, participants are taught that if the customer ever asks, "How much?" in the middle of a presentation, stop and move immediately to close. The intent is to get a signed contract, and the individual is signalling a readiness to buy. The same principle is true in selling ideas. When a decision-maker asks in effect, "How much?" it's time to move to the close, even though the presenter has an hour programmed on the clock. If the decision-maker signals a willingness to accept the idea, go to the close and get the decision, then tell the decision-maker that he has some time left on his schedule. Don't underestimate the value of being able to answer a senior's question as directly and as briefly as possible.

I'LL TAKE CARE OF IT

Reportedly, a young major marched into General George Marshall's office and stated, "General, we have a problem. What shall we do?" The general looked up at him and said, "Major, your job is to present to me a solution to the problem. My job is to decide whether to accept your solution or find me another major." The successful employee will recognize that the boss sees many problems every day. A supervisor values one who can identify a problem, develop a solution, and implement it before it becomes a major issue that the supervisor must handle personally.

An individual looking to advance in the organization should adopt an attitude of, "I'll take care of it." It seems that most people like to bring problems to the senior to resolve. Therefore, subordinates who can take control and resolve problems are very valuable to the organization.

To illustrate how important this trait is: On a business trip to Los Angeles, I was scheduled to co-sponsor a large group at a local hotel. But I was stuck in traffic on the Los Angeles freeway. I called the hotel from a mobile phone to ask a hotel employee to inform the group that I would be late. Although I really did not expect much help from the hotel staff, much to my surprise, a very pleasant, helpful woman answered the phone. When I told her that I would be 20 minutes late and asked if she would relay the information to the group in the room, her response was, "I'll take care of it." I was so taken aback by her directness that I queried again, "Would there be any problem?" She repeated, "Sir, I will take care of seeing that message gets relayed." That so impressed me that I started noticing within my organization how many people were self-starters and would grab the "bull by the horns" and accomplish something that was within their area and ability to achieve. It makes no difference where they are placed in an organization, employees who are self-starters and take on issues, saying, "I'll take care of it and make it happen," are worth their weight in gold to the organization.

DON'T WHINE

Some individuals just cannot resist whining and complaining about the little things, although it obviously will not endear them to their supervisors. When the supervisor has an opportunity to promote or dispense privileges, these little moments of whining will certainly come to mind.

To illustrate: An officer was in charge of providing administrative services to a governmental commission. After the commission had rendered its final report, the officer was asked to prepare an item of appreciation for the Secretary of Defense to give to the commission chairman. The officer griped and whined about having to perform the task. As the officer's senior, I found it easier to prepare the award myself than to deal with the whining; and I lost respect for that individual in the process. If given a job that is a legitimate function of your duties, accept the job and accomplish it to the best of your ability. In the case of the award to the commission, the job got done; but the individual's negative attitude cost him the confidence of his superior.

THE MIKE IS ALWAYS OPEN

As we noted earlier in our discussion of public affairs, leaders are often called to appear before the media to represent the organization. Shortly after my promotion to general officer, the Army's public affairs office "suggested" that I attend an informational session designed to acquaint leaders with how to interface with the news media. In all my years of formal schooling, this short session proved to be the most memorable. Lieutenant Colonel Joe Hollis of the Army's public affairs office came to my office and said, "General, get your coat. I think you will be more comfortable with it." I should have known something was up because it is customary for the military in the Pentagon to work in shirt sleeves. When we arrived at the Pentagon's fifth floor and opened the door to a television studio, a reporter stood ready with a mike in her hand. She was accompanied by a television cameraman. Before I knew it, I was engaged in a live television interview. Forget that we were role playing. As a reporter, she was asking penetrating questions about me, my job, and my personal life. These people had done a good job of preparing, for it was very realistic. Hollis then played back the video to critique my performance. That one session with Hollis was highly informative and had a great impact upon my later contact with the media. It was a good thing, for I would represent the Army many times in live television interviews, background interviews, and before editorial boards, all in addition to making approximately 60 speeches a year, usually with newspaper reporters present.

Hollis taught me, among other things, that there is no such thing as a casual conversation with the media. The leader must always be on the record.

After that initial training session, I found myself going before a television interviewer. As the interviewer was putting the mike on my coat, he asked what I thought of the job performance of then Secretary of Defense Casper Weinberger? The answer to that question has no relevance. Certainly no new brigadier general is going to say anything derogatory about the Secretary of Defense. What is relevant, however, is that I was wearing a live mike. Even though the cameras were not on, the television technicians had started taping my conversation as they were setting up. I later found this is a normal media tactic. People who do not know this end up making some statements they later regret. One should remember that it is the leader's job to represent the organization before the public at large. All leaders should treat every situation as though the mike is always on.

Dealing with the news media can have unusual twists and turns. In the mid-'80s, my daughter, Kathryn Henry, was a television anchorwoman with KWTX in Waco, Texas. She also conducted her own live daily noon talk show. I was the Army's general whose job was to promote the increase of procurement competition with the defense industry. On one of my trips to Texas, she prevailed upon me to be a guest on her show to talk about how the Army buys its goods and services. This event occurred soon after DoD was criticized for paying too much for spare parts. I agreed to be a guest. We did not discuss the questions she would ask me prior to the show. When the show started, she introduced me, not as her father, but as the general from Washington who was there to discuss the Army's buying practices on spare parts. She then turned to me and said, "General, we have heard about the military paying over $400 for an ordinary claw hammer. What is your explanation of this event?" A tough question to be sure. Needless to say, it was a good interview. In the end she acknowledged me as her father, thanking me for coming. The Army later used the tape as an example of how you could find yourself in tough situations—even with your own daughter.

Leaders are called upon to represent the organization before many different groups. Here, we have discussed the news media, but there are others, such as civic organizations and Congress. Leaders must work to develop their interpersonal communication skills so that they can effectively work with others. Remember, prudence dictates that the mike must always be considered "on."

THE POCKET SPEECH

Leaders are often called upon to give speeches. The higher up the individual and the larger the organization, the more speeches the leader will give. This is particularly true in public service. There will be requirements to make public utterances concerning policy or changes in direction. These utterances have the potential for media exposure.

The leader should always have a "hip pocket" speech. Things are going on within every organization that form the basis of a good speech. Three of the top items that are concerning the leader at any time will form the basis for any talk in just about any setting. In corporate settings, new business, backlogs to business, and profits and losses are items of interest to any potential audience. In government, efficiency, streamlining, cost reductions, and job security would all be the basis for a good talk.

The key issue is that leaders are often called on suddenly to say something. If not prepared, they risk the appearance of incompetence.

The first time I encountered such an impromptu situation was in Fort Lee, Virginia. The event was the annual Black History Month. I was a new battalion commander, and I had gone to an evening service at the Army chapel to show support for black history. I was not expecting to give a speech, and I was not prepared to give one. Near the conclusion of the service, the master of ceremonies said, "And we have in the audience the battalion commander, and I'm sure that he would like to say a few words." It caught me totally cold. I made the talk, but never again was I caught short. I developed the "hip pocket" speech. The leader should never go out in public without one.

Even when you are expected to speak, you should always be concerned about maintaining the confidentiality of your notes so that others will not use your material before you have had a chance to do so. An event in Battle Creek, Michigan, reinforced this point and the value of the "hip pocket" speech.

I was scheduled to be the speaker at the Armed Forces Day ceremony, and my public affairs officer had developed a very good Armed Forces Day speech. Generally, I would change speeches to fit my thinking and my speech style, but two very fine public affairs specialists, Linda Stacy Nichols and Earl Nichols (no relation), had worked with me for almost five years and had developed an ability to characterize my speech patterns and write speeches that sounded like what I would give. The speech they gave me was good. I decided to go with it unaltered.

I had developed a habit of having someone place the speech on the podium so I would not have a bundle of papers in my hand as I took my place there. The individual introducing me, a local media consultant, became so engrossed in the introduction that he literally started giving major points of my speech. Not only was he giving points, he was reading substantive paragraphs, word for word, from my speech. It was very disconcerting to have the person introducing me spend 10 of my 20 minutes and present half of my speech. There was no time to rewrite. In fact, there was no time to even reshuffle the pages. So the "hip pocket" speech, framed around what was left of the talk, comprised the Armed Forces Day ceremony speech. (By all accounts, while it may not have been my best speech, it was acceptable.)

There was no ill-intent here, either from the media consultant or my public affairs staff. The working of data and sharing of information brought certain phrases together. The introducing individual had the first opportunity to use them, and he did. But a leader facing this situation will certainly be surprised, and, without an acceptable alternative, embarrassed.

KNOW YOUR AUDIENCE

Of course, even more embarrassing is when people in senior positions forget that they are "selling" to an audience when they deliver a speech. It may be an idea, a concept, a commitment, or a vision. But selling they are, otherwise, they would not be making the presentation in the first place. A common mistake is a "canned" speech with no regard to the interests of the intended audience. The successful politician is able to read the audience and tailor the presentation to meet its expectations. The successful leader should determine beforehand the goals of the speech and the method of delivery that will produce desired results. The result could be anything from the development of a new policy or a different vision to a call for action.

To illustrate how you can really "put your foot in your mouth," consider a presentation conducted shortly after the Clinton Administration took office. A freshman congresswoman from Northern Virginia appeared in her district at Fort Myer, Virginia, to speak to the Association of the United States Army (AUSA) as a luncheon speaker. All that was required in this case was to make a couple of nonoffensive jokes, talk about how the new Congress was going to make things better, and detail how she was going to work for the constituency. She did not do this. She decided that she would try to convince this group of active, retired military, and members of the defense industry that introducing homosexual persons into the military would be a good idea. What you think about the issue is immaterial. The point is that here was an opportunity for her to understand and speak to the audience. Introducing this subject to this audience was tantamount to Daniel walking into the lion's den. After her speech, the consensus was that she had committed a political "no-no." She had alienated a large segment of her own constituency. The issue here is not political. The issue is that at times people miss a golden opportunity to keep their mouths shut on certain subjects. Regardless of your position, it is always advisable to know when to talk and when to keep quiet.

THE FIFTEEN-MINUTE PRESENTATION

With the help of a Pentagon public affairs major, I learned a valuable lesson when I first became a general officer. My first job as Competition Advocate General was to talk to a large group of U.S. senators and representatives and convince them that the Army was increasing competition in its purchasing, and therefore, was meeting the intent and the will of the Congress. The Army's legislative liaison, a very bright and energetic young officer, had set up a breakfast meeting for this talk. Armed with more knowledge than needed on the subject, I spoke to the group and was dismayed to see that, as I was talking, people were getting up and leaving. After the presentation, the major said, "General, about the longest you can keep a congressperson's attention is 15 minutes. (I had taken more than 30.) You might wish to consider limiting any future presentations to that amount of time." What valuable advice. I later found out that it applied not only to congresspersons, but to anyone whose time is critical. (That should include everyone.) I have further refined this thought, and now know that busy people appreciate those who can synthesize information and present it in the shortest possible time. People always appreciate an agenda that moves faster than expected.

Later, when I was in a senior position, people would attempt to get on my calendar for one hour. I resisted an hour's time and later concluded that, regardless of the presentation, anyone could communicate to a decision-maker whatever needs to be submitted with no more than five charts. In one instance, a defense industry senior vice-president did get on my calendar for an hour. After we were in the office with the door closed, and my staff was aware that I was well tucked in for the hour, this senior VP opened an enormous briefcase and pulled out what appeared to be 150 charts. He then proceeded to present and read each chart to me in detail. It was at that point that I concluded that anybody presenting a subject should be able to do so in no more than five charts, and preferably in 15 minutes.

There are, of course, instances where the five-chart or 15-minute presentation may be inappropriate; but the goal to try to achieve these minimums is worthy and will put the presenter in good stead. It takes a little work to be able to condense and build a presentation along these lines, but the emerging leader must recognize the importance of the senior's time and build a concise briefing with logical conclusions. This is important, even when the individual is allotted more time. A concise, tightly organized briefing shows that the individual has it all together and is an individual that the organization should watch for future development.

ANATOMY OF A GOOD SPEECH

Joe Hollis, who became my good friend, was a hard taskmaster. While he was my subordinate, I could ask him a question and consistently get a candid response. If my proverbial "deodorant failed," Hollis would tell me. What a tremendous asset to have in a friend. He had occasion to witness my presentations before large audiences, and I always asked for a critique. He was candid, but in the critique he would offer several points for future consideration. With his consent, I pass these suggestions along.

"First," he said, "good speeches need good humor: a small joke, a simple joke, one that is not offensive. Good speeches need good hand gestures; a public speaker must be animated. For the normal audience, appropriate hand gestures show energy. Develop facial personality; the audience sees the face, and the face has to telegraph the message. If it is wooden, it is going to be a boring speech. The face must be animated and open. Show great candor; audiences want to believe an individual who is leveling with them and 'telling them like it is.' Don't put too much detail into a 15-minute speech. You're not there to make everyone in the room a scholar on your subject. Before a live television camera, use energy; and when you feel like you are making a fool out of yourself, you are just about right. Remember: use short sentences with **lots** of energy."

Hollis' prescription made for some very good speeches.

NEVER BE TOO BUSY FOR YOUR BOSS

As silly as it seems, some employees become so engrossed in their work and their own sense of priorities that they forget that one of the most important functions of their job is to be responsive to their boss. Most people know that their boss is an individual appointed above them in the organization. Even the President of the United States has a boss—the people. The individual who forgets to pay attention to the boss will ultimately suffer disastrous consequences. You only need to look at the one-term presidents of the last few decades to see that losing touch with the "boss" (constituency) places one's future employment in jeopardy.

An employee should develop an ability to get along with peers as well as superiors, otherwise advancement within the organization will be limited. Subordinate leaders will not advance to senior leadership if they cannot understand and deal within the organization. One of the key questions often asked when hiring and promoting is, "Is this person capable of getting along in the organization?" The individual who flunks that test will find closed doors. While such individuals may be professionally and technically competent, they will not be chosen. On the other hand, employees should not pander to or be overly solicitous to the supervisor; but they should be aware that when the leader requests something, they should move without delay to accomplish it. To do otherwise invites negative leadership criticism.

On a lower level, I served with an individual who was the best clothing and textile expert that the Army had developed in over a quarter of a century. This individual, however, had a "personality conflict" with his boss. The textile expert was technically outstanding—four-star generals sought his advice—and he felt that he did not need to defer to his two-star general boss. A mistake! At evaluation time, the two-star general nailed the "expert," and a subsequent board of officers recommended his early retirement based largely upon this evaluation. In my opinion there is no such thing as a "personality conflict" with the boss. Even when an individual feels that a problem is personality driven, it is incumbent upon the individual to get along with the boss. Some employees feel that it is the other way around. This extremely competent clothing and textile individual developed the habit of working very well with all of his boss's bosses, but he was unable to deal effectively with his immediate superior. The result was a career termination.

NEVER PUT UGLY THOUGHTS IN WRITING

Everybody, at some time or another, will experience frustration, disappointment, and even hostility. These emotions may be toward an issue or a person, and sometimes both. Regardless of the situation, never put frustration in writing. Harsh comments are impossible to retract. Then, too, in today's modern age of instant copying, a written epistle will move around the organization with the speed of light. Remember NBC *Today Show* host Bryant Gumble's infamous "memo" in his computer in which he made derogatory comments about his colleagues?

It is incumbent upon the leader to develop a harmonious climate within the organization. The leader may get mad, but ultimately it is the leader who is going to have to "mend the fences." Harsh writing will be hard to mend. One should never, in the heat of anger, write something that is critical of an individual or the group, for surely one will later have to find a way to clean up the results of that document.

It is also best never to say something bad about an individual. If you say it, chances are it will get to the individual you say it about. Sooner or later you will have to make peace if you wish to be productive. These harsh statements about another's character do nothing to enhance the organization. They can only detract from the leader's ability to get things done in the future. Individuals who practice restraint in these matters will find that life is easier within the organizational environment because they do not spend time trying to mend fences.

COMMON SENSE

Successful leaders develop a system of feedback that provides, on a constant basis, a fair and honest appraisal. It is one thing to be technically qualified to do a job, but it is another to have the common sense to make decisions that affect the organization. I know of no school where one can learn common sense. It seems to me that you either have it or you don't. However, smart managers ask for "feedback" on ideas from people whose opinions they respect. Unfortunately, one big drawback of this feedback "sanity check" for some people is that they cannot accept criticism. Some people simply cannot stand to receive bad news. The wise manager must understand that there are times when someone has to be able to walk in and say, "You are wrong, and you ought to reconsider," without having the leader "shoot the messenger." (See also Part II, "Don't Shoot the Messenger.")

NEVER ASSUME CONFIDENTIALITY

Sensitive news is hard to keep and it is difficult, if not impossible, for the leader to be able to tell something of importance to another individual in the organization with the idea that person will maintain total confidentiality. My experience is that the sensitive news will leak and the confidentiality will be lost. I am not speaking of classified government documents security. Surprisingly, these are kept quite confidential. But a thought about a new program or anything that has to do with the human resource aspects of the organization will cause rumors to build very quickly.

Leaders should remember that they are the "hall monitors;" they are in charge of "rumor control." A leader who hears a rumor that is inconsistent with present policy should move very swiftly to set the record straight and tell the organization in clear language what the true position is. The situation is akin to the game of rumor that kids play where one person is told something, whispers it to another, and so on down the line. At the end of the game, the rumor the last person hears is compared with the original rumor. The difference can be surprising. Left unattended, a rumor will take on a life of its own and will be hard to stop unless the leadership does so.

MURPHY'S LAW

Conventional wisdom has it that if it can go wrong, it will go wrong. If there is an event that is important enough to ensure that all goes right, the leader should always check the arrangements and the facilities prior to the event—even if this is to recheck what the action officer has done about the arrangements.

A very personally embarrassing incident occurred when I was cochairman of the Department of Defense Clothing and Textile Board. This board, chartered by the under secretary of defense, comprised industry chief executive officers and the under secretary of defense, himself. At the end of a very successful year, the board reported its progress. The plan was to have the report presented to the under secretary. Lunch would follow at a nearby private club.

A subordinate of mine made the arrangements; and, at the appointed hour, I escorted the group to the club, only to be told that they did not have a reservation for us. When the arrangements were made, the club staff booked this event at their other location—13 miles away! No one had bothered to check the facilities prior to the event. Needless to say, when the group arrived, things were rather hectic. The club worked to correct the mistake; and, while we ended up with a good meal, I was embarrassed by our failure to properly plan and execute.

My lesson was that regardless of one's position, if it is an important event, the individual should ensure that the facilities are checked and the layout of the room is satisfactory. For those who are senior, check with those that are responsible for putting the event on for you. Naturally, the higher up an individual goes in the organization, the less that individual can do personally, so the delegation of this function has to go to someone the leader trusts. The leader should always ask the pertinent questions concerning the event. When in doubt, check and question the event planners to make sure they have done their job.

MOVING UP

Sometimes, organizational leaders decide that they need to move an individual to perform a particular task. Often the leader will go to a subordinate who has impressed the organization and offer a job change. Before declining such an offer, the employee should weigh carefully the facts surrounding the offer. Generally, the organization is saying, "We need help." In such cases the organization and its leaders have been impressed by the individual employee to whom the job is offered. Often, however, the individual employee will stub a toe in handling the job offer. For example: Never reject the offer outright. The job offer probably is not what the employee immediately wants, but chances are the organizational leader is in a better position than the employee to judge the future and the worth of the offer.

A personal example comes to mind. In the early 1980s, I was commander of the mid-western Contract Administration Office in Cleveland, Ohio. I had been there for two years. I was comfortable in the job, and my wife, Sandy, was happy with the house. In short, we liked Cleveland. Lieutenant General Donald Babers, U.S. Army, became the new head of the agency in Washington. Babers was looking for a senior colonel to be his chief of staff. He wanted to focus on improving the procurement process. I received a phone call from a close associate of Babers who told me that the general was coming to Cleveland and was going to offer me the job as his chief of staff. My immediate reaction was that I did not want the job. To be a headquarters staff officer in lieu of a commander is considered by some to be a less important job. I felt, however, that I could not turn Babers down if he offered me the job.

Babers came to Cleveland. He offered. I accepted; and, in looking back, I realize that was the only decision that I could have made that would have advanced my military career. I came to Washington; and, a short time later, I was on the army's promotion list to brigadier general. I believe that if I had stayed in Cleveland and rejected that offer, the short-term gain would have been to stay in Cleveland; but I would not have been recognized by the Army's senior leadership, and, in all probability, I would not have been promoted to general officer.

There are times when one has to carefully weigh the situation. It is usually best to go with the organizational leader's desires rather than depend upon your own wishes.

To illustrate further, I received a call from the under secretary of defense who was looking for a female officer to work as the number two in DoD for small business. The job was to work with widows who had inherited small businesses from their husbands and needed guidance. He asked if I knew of any suitable candidates. I did. In fact, I had two very capable women in my command. I called both officers and notified them of the job opportunity. One chose to interview. The other one declined. The officer who went was selected for the job, and I soon heard that she was doing a dynamite job. The other officer continued to do a good job; but I must admit that, after she refused, I was less impressed with her than before.

The moral here is that when the organization has a need, and the leaders look within to fill that need, the individual that is "tapped" should be very careful before rejecting the offer. Once refused, the leadership may not offer again.

TREATING PEOPLE BETTER

In conversations with senior leaders after they have left a position, one often hears that they regret not treating people better. I've never heard successful leaders comment that they wished that they had been harder on people. The really good leader looks for ways to make people's lives a little easier. The sage advice from those who have gone before is that emerging leaders who really want to make an impact will concern themselves with how to make life easier for subordinates. This does not mean coddling the employees, nor does it mean that the leader does not have to make tough decisions; but it does mean being concerned with the subordinate's well-being.

To demonstrate your commitment to making life better for subordinates, ask subordinates periodically, "Is there anything I can do for you?" It is a simple question, and most will answer, "No, but we thank you for asking." Every now and then, however, the leader will find a situation where this question reveals something of importance about the organization. Always be aware of and concerned about your employees' well-being. Asking this question shows your genuine concern, and acting upon the answers shows true leadership.

BORROWING MONEY FROM EMPLOYEES

Successful leaders know intuitively that they cannot control and direct employees if they borrow anything of value from them. Therefore, never borrow money from employees. In the same vein, never have employees perform personal services unless it is their job. In every organization and in every relationship, there will be times when the leader and the subordinate come to a crucial juncture. There will be times when the leader must tell the subordinate what he wants, and the subordinate will not like it, but must perform. A leader who creates subservience by borrowing money, mixing personal situations with business situations, or asking for unjustified personal services from a subordinate also creates employee resentment and even disrespect, which ultimately severely limit the leader's ability to lead.

CONTEMPORARIES

In the mid-'70s, Georgia Institute of Technology professor Phillip Adler approached me with some advice. "You work very hard at what you do, and you are very good at what you do," he said, "but you have a tendency to upset your contemporaries, big time!" I was flabbergasted. In those midmanagement development years I was working to learn my trade; and when my supervisor gave me a task, I charged ahead to perform that task. Adler's comment was that my success and drive were creating jealousy among my contemporaries. I had recently been assigned to a job normally held by a civil servant two full grades higher than my regular military rank. This position assured me a seat at the table in the staff meeting, and my contemporaries were occupying seats around the side of the room (which is normal in organizational settings). Adler added, "You should develop a way to say something good about your contemporaries and bolster them in the eyes of the leader."

I reflected on what he said and decided to try to improve my standing with my contemporaries. In those instances where I had firsthand knowledge, I would comment to the leader about an individual's performance and assistance in the effort. All comments were honest and straightforward. Nothing was overly flattering, just the pure facts of the situation and the individual's contribution to the effort. The results, however, were dynamic. My relationship with my contemporaries improved, and I learned a very valuable lesson.

Later on, when I was working as the Army's competition advocate general, I had an opportunity to speak about very senior four star generals in glowing terms before the Army's Chief of Staff. I found, as I gave my report concerning the Army's ability to increase competition, that I got more support from these senior generals by complimenting their efforts than I would have had I negatively reported to the Army chief that some of them weren't doing their part. I never had to do that; but, using the Adler technique, I was able to tell the Army's Chief of Staff about the great things that General so-and-so and his organization were doing. Then the Chief of Staff, in conversations with the Army leadership, would mention that I was saying the great things that someone else was doing to increase army purchasing competition. It became apparent that those who did not get the Chief's kudos started trying harder, and things worked very well in the end. In fact, the Army was extremely successful in its efforts during the late 1980s in increasing competition. I concluded that an honest and fair compliment about a contemporary will pay handsome dividends, both professionally and personally.

By the same token, one should never speak ill of a contemporary. Situations generally change, and the parties may find themselves aligned on a subject on which they were previously opposed. This is especially true when one moves up the organizational ladder and the other finds that it narrows close to the top. People who are natural competitors for jobs and positions at the lower end may find themselves allied in positions at the top, one working for the other, and one supporting the other for a senior position in a similar organization. Individuals who "burn their bridges" by walking over the backs of contemporaries will find that ultimately some event will occur, and they will crash and not rise again. On the other hand, individuals who are helpful, although tough competitors and professionally competent, and work as friends will find their reputations with contemporaries enhanced. Developing personal and professional relationships will deter the dirty tricks often associated with political infighting.

THE "SHOOT OUT"

There are times when professionals are working on an issue or issues so sensitive that there will only be a winner or a loser. In this case, the winner should work to ensure that the loser's self-respect is preserved, if possible. The successful leader will look for a way to turn the situation into a win-win. The losers will know that they have lost, but they will appreciate the courtesies extended by the winner.

There was a very tense period regarding DoD acquisition in the Middle East during the Bush Administration. The transfer of contract administration responsibilities was directed by Deputy Secretary of Defense Donald Atwood. What had been performed by the local command would be consolidated into the DCMC. The initial reaction of the senior American general in Saudi Arabia, Major General Thomas Raines, was that he owned everything in the country and was not going to make any transfer. (The further away one gets from the "flag pole," the less one knows about Washington thinking.) Raines did not know that Atwood had a personal interest in the issue, nor did he know that this issue was anything but a "power grab" by some guy back in Washington. His reaction was natural. Had the resistance of those in Saudi Arabia become known to Atwood at the Defense Department, someone would have had some tough explaining to do.

I called on Lieutenant General Jimmy Ross, a friend of both of us, and asked him to send an "Eyes Only" message to Raines explaining the situation. Ross said to him, "I'm coming to you as a friend. You may not know it, but this has the interest of the number-two person in the Defense Department. He has made a decision, you are expected to carry out the decision, and we need your help." As soon as this message arrived, Raines called me and said, "I didn't understand." I told Raines I would take responsibility for the misunderstanding and that I would do everything that I could to ensure that all knew that he was on the team and with the effort. From that point on, Raines carried out the task admirably and with the same intensity as he had when he opposed it at the beginning. I respected him for his abilities and his commitment to his job. He became a winner, and I won my point also. We both were and are thankful for the help of the intermediary (Ross). Raines was later promoted to lieutenant general and continues to serve with distinction.

When issues become decidedly heated and intense, one cannot overlook the value of a third party who can help bring consensus. Once the issue is settled, the winner should do everything possible to ensure that both parties are winners.

FOOT IN MOUTH DISEASE

Sometimes individuals moving up the organizational ladder, feel they can make statements with total impunity. There is an interesting military truism that the things a colonel could say openly and in public would cause trouble if said by a general. Colonels are not considered makers of public policy; generals are, and they always speak for the record.

A colonel who worked for me was promoted to brigadier general, but did not modify his public statements. He had a tendency to make off-color remarks in public. It became so bad that when he would make a speech, I would get phone calls from irate people. In meetings, he had the habit of telephoning his immediate superior on the speaker phone and, with an audience listening, attempt to force a favorable decision from him. All too often I found that I would have to override him in front of his subordinates. Eventually, I asked him to report to me in my office for a heart-to-heart talk. I said, "Every time you open your mouth, you put your foot in it; and you must not suffer from foot and mouth disease any longer." After that meeting he did improve. Despite this testy but necessary conversation, we are still friends today.

A senior official is expected to make public statements consistent with good public policy. Making public statements has an impact on the organization and also reflects on the individual. Leaders are supposed to do the right thing at the right time.

BAD FACTS . . . BAD DECISIONS

In law school, I was taught that bad facts make for bad laws. As a manager/leader, I've come to believe that the same principle applies—bad facts make for bad management decisions. The leader needs to be aware that there will come a time when, through either awe, envy, or fear, subordinates will not confess their true feelings.

Dr. Jerry Harvey of George Washington University has a theory that groups have a hard time dealing with consensus. He calls it the "Abilene paradox." The paradox surrounds a Texas family who, in the middle of summer in the 1950s, decided to drive 60 miles to Abilene in a car that wasn't air conditioned to eat at a cafeteria. Everyone agreed to go. They went and returned mid-afternoon during the heat. It was a miserably hot experience. After they returned, they all pointed fingers at each other for fostering the original idea. Harvey's point is that all agreed to go, all had a miserable time, and then, when they got back, all asserted that they did not want to go in the first place. This is the "Abilene paradox."

When I first heard Harvey, I was amused at the story; but I later became aware that he was correct in his assertion that organizations suffer from the same malady. Once the leader focuses on a specific objective, there are those within the organization who will follow, even when they do not believe in the project. This can be negative or beneficial for the leader. Leaders who seek organizational change must ensure that they are getting the best advice. Generally, change is successful because the organization truly wants to do what the leader has asked them to do. But, there will always be those who do not wish to change, for they like the status quo and will resist a certain amount of change at almost any cost. Therefore, not all will be 100 percent behind the project. Assuming that the leader is not a person that the organization simply detests, there will be enough people granting support and wanting to make the project work. That is generally good for leaders, but it does place a significant responsibility on them to ensure that they are not going off "half cocked" with half-baked ideas that will expend organizational resources needlessly. Leaders must accept the responsibility to make sure that they get good, honest feedback from responsible people who can advise as to the outcome and the benefits of the projects.

General Carl Vuono, U. S. Army Chief of Staff during Desert Shield/Storm, had many advisors who were giving him true, honest appraisals regarding the war's operation, especially from a logistical point of view. The result was America's finest logistical hour.

Today's leaders must deal with the complexities of both organizational and human resources. They must seek sound advice and must know when the advice they are receiving is nonbiased, executable, and a benefit to the organization. To do otherwise invites proof of the adage that bad facts make for bad management decisions.

DEAL WITH THE PROBLEM

One of the easiest problems to resolve, and often for the leader one of the most difficult to execute, is effectively handling animosity, either toward the leader or toward the organization. The leader should not let an adverse situation fester, for it never gets better with age. Perception is reality, and the leader should treat grievances as though they were real.

Often aides and subordinates with incomplete information speak for the leader, when they haven't checked the facts out. This will sometimes cause a "situation" between the leader or the organization and another leader or organization. I've never seen such a situation where, unless there was an overt leadership act, the situation improved by itself. Most situations can be forgiven and maybe even forgotten, but not without recognizing the varying personalities leaders present. Some are self-absorbed. Others are not so temperamental. All leaders have unique characteristics, and leaders who have been slighted will have their psyches bruised. The successful leader understands that if a situation occurs that is not really critical but could get in the way of future relationships, the soundest approach is to work out the issue with the other leader before it becomes a major problem.

To dramatize how a small event can become major thorn: I had just taken over as a battalion commander at Fort Lee, Virginia, in the late 1970s, and I met a sergeant first class. As we talked, I noticed a string that was loose on the sergeant's uniform. (In the military, loose strings are not appropriate.) I reached up and pulled the string. I thought I was doing the sergeant a favor by removing the string and thought nothing more of it. I left and returned to my headquarters.

Soon my battalion sergeant major told me that we had an incident on our hands. It seems that the sergeant felt that I had embarrassed him by removing the string. By this time the entire NCO corps at the post was buzzing with the issue that this lieutenant colonel had embarrassed the sergeant by pulling a string off of his uniform. It may sound like a small issue, but at the time it was a major problem. The NCO corps thought that I should apologize and make amends. Those around me felt that a lieutenant colonel should not have to stoop so low as to apologize to a lower ranking NCO. By the time the word got to me, the entire post was talking about the incident. My response was immediate. "If I have embarrassed the sergeant, I owe him an apology—let's go." I went to see the sergeant. I told him that I had not intended to embarrass him. It was just a natural reflex for me to pull the string as one would flip off a piece of lint. Immediately he accepted the apology. The situation was defused and forgotten. The sergeant and I had a unique bond for the rest of the time we served together at the Army post. I tell this story, not because of the way I handled it, but because the lesson to me was that a situation will escalate unreasonably if not properly and quickly addressed.

In the end it makes no difference who is at fault. The key is to resolve the issue before it gets out of hand and let the parties focus on more substantive issues.

PERSONAL INTRODUCTION

One of the simplest and often unused methods for a subordinate to keep his name before a senior is to immediately introduce himself. "Hello, sir or ma'am. I'm John Doe." This is especially true for the senior officials of large corporations or in the military. In my last military job, I had people located all over the world. Approximately 20,000 people were under my direct command. While I tried, it was impossible for me to remember every person, but even those that I was able to remember, I generally would associate with a particular place. If I saw someone who was not at the place I associated them with, I had difficulty recalling the name. Added to this, like many leaders, I was often in situations where many people were already present, expecting me to instantly recall the names of all those who came to shake hands. And, worst of all, the person that anyone has difficulty with is the one they have not seen in a long time who says with a smiling face, "Bet you don't know who I am."

This type of game is dreaded. It places the leader, or anyone else, in an awkward spot. Unless the leader instantly recalls the name, it only leads to embarrassment on both sides. On the other hand, the individual who walks up to the leader and states, "Sir, I'm John Doe, I live in Los Angeles, work at so-and-so, and it's good to see you again," creates a favorable situation (and impression). One thing leaders become adept at over a period of time is listening and constantly assessing information about who an individual is, where the individual lives and works, and if they have ever met before. You will never be wrong to introduce yourself to a senior immediately upon meeting. The reverse of that is not always the case, so why take the gamble? Make the most favorable impression.

DON'T TAKE ON THE KING

It is often interesting to watch subordinates in the presence of their superiors. There are those who feel that their importance will be magnified if they can show the boss how smart they are and how stupid he or she is. It is hard to believe, but I have observed this many times. However, I have never seen this tactic work to the subordinate's benefit. Most of the time, it works to their detriment.

There was a story years ago about the young major who would make continuous corrective observations in staff meetings. His general admonished him on more than one occasion to stop this practice. The major still pressed his point and once said to the general, "I'm sure you didn't make general by keeping your mouth shut." The general thought for a moment, and responded, "No, you're right. But that sure is how I made lieutenant colonel."

There will be times when, in a large meeting, the superior will, through incomplete or erroneous facts, arrive at the wrong decision. This is not the time for a subordinate to jump up and say, "That is the dumbest decision I have ever heard." It is best to accept the decision and then look for the opportunity to approach the senior privately. (That is assuming the senior has not given an order that has to be carried out immediately.)

A subordinate should never confront a senior before a large audience. There are ways to set the record straight and have the leader reconsider the decision. One can request a private meeting or send a note to the senior, to be opened only by him, marked personal and confidential. If the senior does not know the facts, the staff has failed to properly brief that leader. Leaders want to make the right decisions; and organizations do not want to, nor should they, make decisions based upon misstatements of facts. However, this is not the issue. The issue is how to deal with the leader who has made a bad decision based upon factual error or misapplication of the facts. If attempts to reach the leader through a one-on-one meeting or a personal note fail, then look for the associate closest to the leader and take the facts to this individual so the associate can approach the leader. In the end, a leader appreciates the subordinate who sets the record straight, but knows how to do it in a manner that does not embarrass the leader in front of others.

WATCH FORMALITIES

In the military, formalities are a part of life. Senior officers call sergeants "Sergeant So-and-so." Subordinates always refer to senior officers as "Colonel So-and-so," "General So-and-so." That particular culture is pretty well established. In the commercial world, it is acceptable for seniors and subordinates to call each other by their first names. However, there are always times when one should be aware of the situation and refer to the senior official by their title. Custodians generally do not refer to the corporation's board chairman in formal settings as "Bill." By the same token, even in the military, members of the same rank refer to others by title, for example general or colonel. Even in answering the telephone, military staff often answer by title; for example "Colonel Jones." Today, however, a certain amount of informality is accepted.

In dealing with the defense industry, the colonels working for me would often refer to the senior CEOs of major defense firms as "John," "Dick," or "Bill." My comment to them is that they should refer to these individuals as they would in the military. If a colonel is dealing with the CEO of a major corporation, he or she should refer to the CEO as "Mr. Jones" or "Mrs. Doe" rather than by first name. It is inconsistent to call yourself general and refer to the CEO as "Jim."

The same principle applies when a junior officer deals with the wife of a senior officer. While the wife of a senior officer will often say to the junior officer, "Call me Jane," there are times when referring to her as "Jane" would be inappropriate. Service schools do not train junior officers about this etiquette. The key here is that a junior officer would never be wrong referring to the wife of the senior officer as "Mrs. Jones." The practice of calling her on the telephone and saying, "Jane, this is Captain So-and-so," is inconsistent. If the junior wishes to remain formal, he could call the senior's wife and say, "Mrs. Jones, this is Captain Smith," or he could call and say, "Jane, this is John Smith." Either would be correct.

The military has changed substantially in the past 30 years. When I first entered the military, no one would ever think of calling the senior officer's wife by her first name, and the senior officer's wife probably would never suggest that a junior do so. Today's spouse, rightfully so, generally is more informal than yesteryear's. However, there are certain rules that the subordinate should apply, even though it may be considered old fashioned. Good manners are never out of style, in the military or in the business world.

TREAT YOUR EMPLOYEES WITH RESPECT

At times all supervisors will become frustrated. Job pressures will become intense. The issue is how does a supervisor deal with job pressures and employee relationships? Everyone has seen the supervisor who is "quick on the trigger" and willing to take someone to task for minor misdeeds. I asked a group of middle- to low-management employees to name a major negative leadership characteristic. The answer overwhelmingly was supervisors who discipline or berate their employees in view of others.

PRAISE

If an employee makes a mistake or does something that is disagreeable, a senior should never speak harshly to the employee in public. The old adage, praise in public, condemn in private, has great application; and, if followed, will allow managers and leaders to administer more efficiently. It should be easy to praise others, but some leaders find it difficult. I believe, however, that regardless of an employee's actions, a leader will never enhance the organization nor improve efficiency by condemning a subordinate in an open hearing. This task is better suited for a one-on-one meeting in a private place where the individual does not suffer public disgrace. In my experience, when an employee has been "chewed out" in public, the embarrassment over this incident will be remembered long after the reason for it has been forgotten.

It would be nice, of course, if every supervisor acted benevolently and didn't "fly off the handle" when something went wrong. However, supervisors come in all sizes, shapes, and dispositions, and, though one would like to keep an even disposition, even those who do act quickly and harshly know who they are and generally wish they could change. This is one leadership characteristic that, if displayed, should be changed if the leader really hopes to gain employee acceptance and have an organization willing to be led. Under no condition, should a person discipline an employee in the presence of others.

If any superior in a moment of anger or frustration, verbally abuses a particular employee in the presence of others, the supervisor in every case will be the loser. T remaining work force will develop great sympathy for the employee receiving the verbal admonishment, even if that employee is not the most liked.

The first time this happened to me was in Germany in the early 1960s. I was in my office with my sergeant. My immediate boss walked into my office, which I shared with a subordinate, threw a paper on my desk, and started to verbally abuse me about the contents. I remember the humiliation of being "chewed out" in front of a subordinate. Over the years observing other similar situations, I have never seen an instance when the situation was improved after an employee is bawled out in front of others. In fact, I believe it becomes worse, for this issue will continue to fester when all other issues are settled.

On the other hand, simple praise and a pat on the back or a warm word in front of others will do wonders, not only for the receiving individual, but for the rest of the work force. While some may be envious, all will feel good about the supervisor making the gesture.

WE ARE ALREADY DOING THAT

There are times when the leader gives direction to individuals. In most cases, individuals are working on the issue. The employee who responds to the leader's guidance with the words, "We are already doing that," is making a grave mistake. In giving the guidance, leaders are thinking about the issue. They are telling which way they want the organization and this project to proceed. It is obvious that the progress has not been satisfactory, or there would have been no need for the conversation.

The employee who responds to the leader's guidance with, "We are already doing that," is foreclosing any future discussion and is sending a very strong message that as soon as the leader departs, the guidance will not be followed. At least not in the spirit of the leader's intentions. What appears to be an innocent statement results in a negative reaction from the boss. The leader will think, "They cannot carry my directive forward with the energy that I want to see on this project if this person is telling me now, after I have just reviewed the situation, that `we are already doing that.' It is obvious they are not doing it well or I would not have suggested the approach." Therefore, to any employee, regardless of position in the organization, if your superior suggests that an issue be accomplished, the proper response should be, "Yes, Sir. We'll take that as an action. We'll work the issues, pros and cons, and we will return to you for a review." This approach conveys action and is preferable even though the organization may indeed already be embarked on the course directed by the leader.

PERSONAL ATTRIBUTES

One of the key traits that I **always** looked for in a subordinate when I was giving direction is note-taking. In the majority of cases, individuals who take notes are the same individuals who accomplish tasks. Conversely, the individuals who do not take notes are those who forget instructions. This failure to attend to detail is a fatal personal mistake, for the higher one moves in an organization, the more demanding the requirements. Senior leaders do not like to repeat instructions. Since there are enough good employees who can accomplish the task with one set of instructions, why would a leader put up with one who requires repeated instructions because of forgetfulness or failure to follow through? The simple answer is to get an employee who can do it the first time and get rid of those who cannot. Harsh, but a reality. In my case, if I found that I had to ask an individual again about a particular subject, I was less than impressed with the employee's performance on the job. Simply stated, all employees should react to specific instructions from the leader without the leader having to remind them.

At the senior levels in the Pentagon, an official in a meeting will have a secretary recording the requests; and, after the meeting, a paper will come out telling what actions are required and who is responsible. In smaller organizations, the leader would simply say to an employee, "I need to know the answer to question X." It is the employee's duty to remember this task and to go about accomplishing it. Failure to remember the task is a cardinal breach of business and organizational responsibilities.

Employees who develop note-taking habits will find that they are more productive. A simple technique I used is to keep 3 x 5 inch blank cards in my hip pocket. Rather than carrying a book, and at times not having it with me, I was always able to have a piece of paper ready for jotting notes. Most of the notes that I made for this manuscript were recorded on those 3 × 5 cards. Another technique is Lieutenant General Chuck McCausland's habit of taking a small, spiral, grade-school notebook with him to all meetings. He would only record pertinent points and, for any meeting, would have no more than a small paragraph of notes. The paragraph would contain any task that he had picked up from the meeting.

It does not matter what process you use. You might have your own. What does matter is developing early on a habit of making notes of tasks and actions to which you are required to respond. Then by all means set about to accomplish the task.

COMPETITION

Whether you like it or not, it is very difficult to go through a career without being subjected to an element of competition. Employees are in competition with other employees for opportunities to grow, for promotions, and for new jobs. We are generally in competition with others to generate more business or to sell our products. Competition is what Americans value in the business and organizational structure.

For the better part of 25 years, I have been an avid participant in competitive sports—primarily squash and racquetball. I have drawn a correlation between performance in a game and performance on the job. I'm not suggesting that you need to be an avid sports enthusiast to be successful in your professional career, but I am advancing the notion that there are some similarities between success in competitive sports and success in a career. I believe that the difference between winning and losing is around five percent. If two players are equally capable, have similar physical conditioning, and play with an equal ability to handle the racket, golf club, or bat; they will on a particular day perform very similarly. The difference is the mental desire to win—the ability to plan and develop a better strategy than the other.

The same can be said for those in organizational endeavors. Those who practice their professions, have the technical skills, are educated, and work at fine-tuning these skills will be considered technically competent. What then distinguishes one person from the other? In sports it always comes down to a final throw, putt, or point. In business and organizations, the issues are similar but a little more blurry. The basic point is that there is only about a five percent difference between winning and losing in both athletics and business.

If one accepts this notion, then the next question must be, "What does one need to do to be in the 5 percent winner's group"? It could be what I call the "X" factor. The "X" factor implies that a person who is physically fit and technically competent in competition with another physically fit and technically competent individual will need the "X" factor in order to be victorious. The "X" factor is mental. It is that inner strength that one obtains in the final moment that keeps the pressure and focus on the issue. Often in sports when behind, I mentally say, "I did not come to lose." I may be behind in points, but I try to focus on the next point to display my competence and to be mentally smart. Another way to say it is to keep your eye on the ball and your mind focused on the rally. The winner at this point is the one who can stay mentally focused. I believe the "X" factor is the mental discipline that a person can exert to an issue. The difference between victory and second best is small. The individual who can master the art of mentally focusing on a particular situation and being persistent will be successful more times than not.

Footnote: Nothing here should be construed to mean "dirty deeds." True awards go to the honest sportsman and the one who projects honest organizational business dealings. I speak to focusing on objectives and using your abilities to achieve a desired result. All this is in the spirit of honest competition. Unfair competition has no place either in sports or in the board room, office, or factory.

SOCIALIZING

Humans are sociable creatures. Social creatures like to get together in nonbusiness type of arrangements. Employees who feel that they have been hired only to perform professional business and that their social life is totally their own can maintain that separation. However, you could make the case that individuals who assert that they are not going to be a part of the social climate will not rise high in the organization. Always consider that if the organization or the leader sponsors a social event, the employees should attend. It is not required to go to every social event, but it is in good form to attend a respectable number to show support for the leader and the organization.

In the military there has been a major change in attitude in the past 30 years. Regulations attempt to prohibit supervisors from requiring employees to attend social events. This is true for legal purposes, but I have never known a senior officer who gave a party who did not notice those subordinates who supported it and those who did not. Not surprisingly, those who support the boss are looked upon with favor, and those who habitually do not get a "raised eyebrow"; and, I think, will receive only those benefits and considerations that are nondiscretionary. The point is that, if the leadership has a social function, support from the organization's members is important to the leader and will be appreciated.

Washington is a city known for its social events. Arriving politicians soon learn that they needn't stay long at an event, but they need at least to make an appearance. Then they are free to leave. It is also a must to claim your name tag because it indicates that you were invited, accepted, and attended. (You should pick up your name tag because most sponsoring organizations determine no-shows by the ones that are not retrieved.) Failure to do so has a negative connotation.

The same holds true for organizational social events. You should plan to go to a majority of functions to which you are invited. You can stay a respectable time and then pay your respects to the senior officer and the host before leaving. In past generations in the military, no one ever left a party before the senior officer. It is still a good idea to keep an eye on the senior, but today, with both spouses working and children in school, it is acceptable to attend and leave after paying respects to seniors and hosts.

To the senior officials: You may be having the best time at the party, but there will be those who will not leave until you have departed. A senior officer should always leave a social function a little earlier than normal. This practice gives the host an opportunity to say "good night" to the remaining guests.

A good rule of thumb when in a new job, situation, or city is always to attend the first social event you are invited to. If you refuse later invitations, everyone will think that you have a good excuse. If you refuse the first invitation and also refuse the second or subsequent invitations, people will assume that you are not a team player—that you are anti-social. You will be talked about.

Bottom line on organizational social events: attend, enjoy, pay respects to the host and senior, and depart at leisure. If you are the senior official present, don't stay too long.

THE BENEVOLENT LEADER

Earlier, we spoke of two types of leaders—the fire-eating dragon and the benevolent leader. I am convinced that the benevolent leader will be more successful over the long run. Here is why.

It has been said that it is lonely at the top. Certainly it is true that ultimately the responsibility of all that the organization does or fails to do lies on the shoulders of the leader. If you are not willing to accept this responsibility, you should not aspire to leadership. Leaders cannot delegate or otherwise absent themselves from the responsibility of what their organizations do or fail to do. Some leaders readily accept the responsibility with verbiage, but not with actions. This leads some people to see leaders as those who do not do heavy lifting, work entirely inside, and live a pretty cushy existence. They go to meetings, listen to the presentations of others, and review the written work of the staff. Yet what is often overlooked is that although leaders can delegate authority, they can never delegate responsibility. The leader remains responsible for decisions and their ultimate success or failure. You don't rise in leadership without concluding that in any organization problems are inevitable.

Things happen in organizations that require attention. If this were not so, there would be no need for a leader. Therefore, the leader who does not create a climate of open communication of both the positives and the negatives is doing a disservice to the organization and becomes, in my opinion, an ineffective leader.

Conversely, the leader who creates a warm climate that, in effect, says, "If you have an issue, I'm approachable," will find that goodwill will permeate through the organization, and the organization will respond positively. This does not mean that the leader is going to work the issues of the organization. But, it does mean that when an issue is important enough to require the leader's personal intervention, the organization's members will feel that they have an approachable leader who can accept news easily.

I've known so-called leaders who could not control their emotions. These are well qualified and professionally competent people, but the first time an employee relays bad news and the leader explodes, the entire organization experiences a chilling effect. In some cases, it will be the last time an individual voluntarily informs the leader about a problem. The next time there is an issue that deserves the leader's attention, it will lay on the desk of a subordinate until it has become unmanageable. The leader loses because, in stifling open communication, he or she has lost the opportunity to work the problem in a timely manner.

To be truly successful, leaders must be accessible, and they must deal with staff in such a way that they feel the leader can be trusted to receive information without turning on the individual who brought the news.

BODY LANGUAGE

Leaders should be aware that since they are in public view 24 hours a day, they must be conscious of body language. Leaders are expected to exude confidence. This is particularly true in military situations. I recall in March of 1972 the North Vietnamese had launched a major military offensive into South

Vietnam. I was a major at the time and went to see my general about bringing more American supplies in to shore up the South Vietnamese government. The general seated at his desk looked very tired and drawn. I explained why I was there. As I left, I was thinking that his physical demeanor and his body language did not inspire my confidence.

The same applies to a leader in any endeavor. My daughter, Kathryn, tells a similar story about when she was in the television industry. Her producer, when things went wrong, had a nervous habit of hunching his shoulders and wringing his hands. It was obvious to all that this leader was distressed, and his actions did not inspire the confidence of his work force that he was capable of making the right decisions for the group. Be aware of your body language and try to convey a positive attitude, despite how you might feel physically or emotionally at the moment.

AS AN ASIDE

A flag officer's aide once told me that it is preferable not to be an aide to an unmarried superior. Marriage has a way of equalizing one's faults. The single executive becomes consumed with pursuing a career and often will work subordinates to exhaustion. Often, the unmarried leader does not display an adequate regard for the subordinate's family life. While a few instances of "let's work overtime" are satisfactory, especially during emergencies, the unmarried leader tends to require this on a regular basis.

When I assumed command of the battalion at Fort Lee, Virginia, in 1978, I left my family in Atlanta, Georgia, so that my son could complete the school year. I was full of vigor and wanted to get into the job and start things as fast as I could. Since I was without my family, I had no reason to go home in the evening, so I tended to overwork. While this was enjoyable to me, I failed to realize that I was pushing the organization too hard. After a few weeks of this type of activity, my very wise command sergeant major suggested that there were others in the organization that had families, and it would be nice if they could spend some time with them. This was a good point I learned from him.

Senior executives should consider subordinates' families and their well-being as part of the organizational setting. If subordinates are content in their family responsibilities, they are better employees and will be more productive on the job. Leaders should assume the responsibility to make sure that the demands they place upon the employees allow them to balance the duties of their jobs with the needs of the family.

SPORTS REVEAL CHARACTER

You can tell a lot about the character of a person while observing that person playing a sport. If people will cheat in sports, chances are they will cheat in business. It is basic to honesty, and honesty goes with those who play sports. Everyone who plays golf knows the rules, but within golf there are a lot of opportunities to defy those rules—take an extra mulligan (free shot) or move your ball. It is difficult to think that a person who will "fudge" the truth in sports will be 100 percent honest in business or other relationships. Some executives, prior to employing an individual, will take that person on a sports outing to observe character.

The same can be said about temper. People who lose their tempers uncontrollably in sports will lose it uncontrollably in business. It seems that in sports, people let their guard down and commit certain practices and display anger when they would not normally do so.

Sports offer the opportunity to observe an individual's true character. What you see in the sporting arena will ultimately be the same characteristics that are displayed in the business setting.

HAVE A PROSPECTIVE EMPLOYEE DRIVE THE CAR

Successful leaders want to employ people of vision who can think and plan farther than the case at hand. A friend of mine uses the technique of observing a prospective employee as the individual is driving a car. If the person is watching only the car ahead in traffic and not paying attention to what is happening four to five cars ahead, then this person will be shortsighted in business, only looking at the instant and not toward the future. If a prospective employer invites you to drive, chances are you are being tested to determine whether or not you have the vision to plan, organize, and direct multiple functions. The leader is observing how you drive and whether or not you are able to anticipate situations that are happening far ahead, rather than close by.

TAKING OVER NEW DUTIES

A leader taking over a new position needs to keep an open mind about the new organization. As a new leader, don't be compromised by those who get to you first with their thoughts and previous dispositions. I have seen situations where personalities became polarized on a subject. A new leader comes to take over the organization, and employees will work hard to convince the new leader of the merits of their view to maintain the status quo. Since these issues and employee positions are based upon personality and interpersonal relationships, they will almost always get in the way of the issues the leader wants to address. If the leader simply accepts these views, all that has happened is that the organization traded one leader for another. The employees have taught the new leader to continue in the same direction the organization was already headed.

I became aware of this organizational tendency in the early 1980s. Prior to taking over the Detroit, Michigan, contract administration operation, I started receiving position papers from the employees of my new organization. At this point I had not met anyone associated with my new assignment. The previous leader had been totally ineffective. It appeared that he spent most of his time reading the *Wall Street Journal* and taking care of personal business. His deputy became the de facto decision-maker and ran the day-to-day operation. Detroit had at one time been a co-equal organization to the Cleveland operation, and there were some who resented being subordinate to Cleveland. Therefore, many turf fights ensued.

Two weeks prior to staring the job, I started receiving communications posturing about the merits of the various employees' positions. On the way to Detroit, I decided to stop off in Cleveland and meet my new superior. This proved to be the right decision. I was able to establish a personal and professional relationship not only with my new boss, but also with the higher headquarters employees. When I got to Detroit, I met some equally competent employees who were subordinate to me. The feeling between the two staffs, however, was not good; and I soon concluded that, unless we could get things in harmony, all business issues would fail. There had to be an outside catalyst. I became that catalyst.

The Cleveland headquarters, lacking confidence in the Detroit operation, had issued a directive that changed the boundaries and reduced the influence of Detroit. Cleveland did not feel that Detroit was responsive to them. After observing this situation, my reaction was to go back to Cleveland and tell my new boss that the relationships between our staffs were so bad that we needed to work this issue first. I requested that he hold off on the decision to re-allocate boundaries and give me 30 days to work the issue. I also requested that he instruct his staff to quit bad-mouthing the Detroit operation. He agreed.

I returned to Detroit after my initial get-together with the people. I assured the Detroit staff that I was impressed with their competence and capabilities, but that we had to work to quit bad-mouthing the Cleveland operation. The Cleveland headquarters was our superior, and we were going to take directions from Cleveland from this point on. I then went back to Cleveland and told the Cleveland staff that we came with peace and that in the future we would work in harmony. To be successful, I personally needed the Cleveland staff to work with

me. The tactic worked. It worked because the leader must set
the climate and the tone of what is expected. The problem was
that these two organizations had fought with each other over
many years on a professional basis. It was the leader's job to define how future relationships would be conducted. Both organizations responded quite favorably; and, in the end, Detroit
became a high producer and a contender for best subordinate element awards.

From a leadership point of view, there was a lot of pressure
on me to assume and adopt each organization's position.
Leaders find themselves answering these questions. The field
will say to the leader, "Are you a field-type leader?" The staff will
say to the leader, "Do you respect and will you protect your
staff?" There will be tremendous pressure to choose between
the two, but the leader must resist this trap. Leadership cannot
be effective if the organization buttonholes the leader into either
position. The leader is the leader of both staff and field, and
must make absolutely sure that each understands and appreciates that the staff works to assist the leader in implementing
policy, and the field executes that policy. To pick and choose between these two elements will defeat the leader's goals.

NEGOTIATIONS—"WHAT DO WE NEED TO DO TO MAKE THIS WORK?"

Too often, in negotiations, one party will place the burden
on the other party to solve the issue. Statements such as, "We
can't do this because regulations preclude this approach," or,
"The senior leadership will never accept this type of action," in-
hibit successful negotiation. One of the best ways to continue
negotiations on a subject is to very politely continue to ask the
other party, "I'd like to make this happen. What do we need to
do to make it happen?"

Surprising how this statement, which is nonthreatening,
considers a cooperative approach. When things get to a stale-
mate, one party looks at another and says, "I want to do this.

How can we make this happen?" This removes obstacles and it places both parties in a position to constructively work toward a successful agreement. Biased statements such as, "My people will never accept this," or, "This is an insult for you to offer," are all counter-productive. What is productive, though, is the earnest feeling that you want to make the agreement and make the deal. How do we go about solving this dilemma? What do we need to do to move this toward a deal? This focuses the energies on those issues that are precluding an agreement, and it enables both parties to work toward that agreement.

HEAR IT TWICE, IT'S IMPORTANT

One thing that I have observed with senior staff at all echelons, both in government and industry, is that if a senior leader ever makes a statement twice, it is important. Subordinates can bet that they will hear it again in the form of a requirement for action. The savvy employee is one who, when hearing a statement twice, attempts to get a handle on the issue. The higher individuals go in the hierarchy of leadership, the less they like to repeat directives and guidance. The employee who appears to read the boss's mind will be one step ahead in organizational success.

SCOPE OF AUTHORITY

Don Yockey, former Under Secretary of Defense for Acquisition, in addressing a group of senior executives at the Washington-based Procurement Round Table, commented, "A leader can deal with any problem as long as the boss backs you up." He was referring to problems that the United States was having in developing and producing the C-17 airlift that the U.S. Air Force so desperately wants and the Army so urgently needs.

Yockey's statement is true at all levels of management. Subordinates need to know the bounds of their authority. The leader needs to give the subordinate the authority to deal successfully with the issues. When Secretary of the Army John Marsh appointed me as the Army's first competition advocate general, the Army Chief of Staff General John Wickham, said to me in our first meeting, "Chuck, you have an important job to do, and it will be hard. I want you to move out and do the job; don't be concerned about your career. Come and see me every 90 days and tell me how it is going. When the Army leaders know that you have my support, you will get theirs." What wonderful guidance and commitment. Wickham was indeed correct. His support of my mission was the one most important attribute in the Army's successful effort to increase competition in procurement.

To the contrary, many careers are cut short because individuals operate outside the scope of their authority and the senior "loses confidence" in the individual. In Washington politics, when this situation occurs, the individual becomes the "walking dead"; and it is normally only a short time before the employee departs for various reasons.

The key here is that the first rule of survival in a leadership role is for subordinate leaders to obtain and recognize the true scope of their authority. Failure to do so is often fatal to a career. The senior leader should then develop the boundaries so that the subordinate leader understands fully the scope of responsibilities.

PART
IV

HENRY'S FINAL POINTS ON LEADERSHIP

I have been fortunate in a long military career to have held a variety of management and leadership positions. I have been equally fortunate in the mentors I have encountered, the wise and benevolent leaders I have been associated with, and even the not-so-wise leaders I have been able to observe. From these leadership experiences and associations, I was able to learn and develop the principles I have set forth in this book. Here, I try to synthesize these principles into a concise set of guidelines on leadership. I call them "Henry's Points on Organizational Leadership" and "Henry's Points on Individual Leadership."

HENRY'S POINTS ON ORGANIZATIONAL LEADERSHIP

The leader must:
- first determine the true mission and purpose.
- work for employee "buy in."
- create a sense of urgency.
- develop and present a clear vision to the organization.
- be ethically driven.
- involve customers as early as possible.
- involve employees in all phases of change.
- tell people what is going on—fully, clearly, concisely, and continuously.
- speak with one voice, and be seen as one face to the organization.
- establish and empower those involved with change early in the process.
- develop early and issue a clear vision of success to the organization.
- practice what he or she preaches.
- demand professionalism, honesty, integrity, and fairness.
- personally develop and issue long- and short-term plans to the organization.

- foster and encourage "we and us" thinking.
- provide leadership consistent with the goal.
- maintain a consistent purpose.
- be accountable, but delegate authority.
- involve supporting organizations and make them partners.
- recognize emotional issues (both people and organizational) and deal with them positively.
- ask often what the organization does well or poorly, what needs changing, and what needs to be left alone?
- not shoot the messengers.
- recognize and address the question, "Why do it?"
- recognize the final goal by getting everybody working toward it.
- maintain customer focus.
- continuously recognize superstars, both individuals and teams, and help them move ahead.
- be a strong mentor.
- forge new avenues and support innovative thinking (both from self and subordinates).
- develop new thinking and definition within the process.
- instill individual commitment to continuous process improvement.
- market organizational efforts and successes to others in decision-making authority.
- be upfront and early in recognizing cultural differences within and outside the organization; then address diverse issues openly.
- deal with people issues—rapidly, openly, fully, and honestly.
- understand and deal with bureaucratic thinking and organizational mindlock by bashing the bureaucracy!
- when making a mistake, "fess up."
- know that government and bureaucracies do not relate to a profit and loss statement, although they should.

- know that it is not enough to develop an action plan. It has to be implemented. And the key is to "follow up."
- know that eliminating waste creates "best value."

HENRY'S POINTS ON INDIVIDUAL LEADERSHIP

- To some, it is not substance but form that necessarily carries the day, but substance will prevail over the long term.
- The individual who develops interpersonal skills and confidence will perform better than someone who may know the subject matter but is unable to effectively communicate.
- If the leadership is concentrating solely on reducing cost, then all other factors become secondary.
- Abusing subordinates has no positive effect on the organization at any time.
- Leaders must define what the organization does well and what it does poorly.
- Separate the bad news of the issue from the people involved in the issue.
- The more effort a leader places on promoting the worth of subordinates and enhancing their capabilities and attributes, the greater the dividends to both.
- The time expended in communicating with employees pays handsome dividends.
- One of the most important leadership tools is to give authority and responsibility to the worker at the lowest organizational level.
- Accepting both responsibility and authority is an essential element of successful leadership.
- It is important that the leader keep the energy level up by being positive and enthusiastic.
- For the junior aspiring to senior positions, now is the time to think about personal conduct.

- Loyalty will not guarantee success; however, disloyalty will never be forgotten.
- Although leaders can delegate authority, they cannot delegate or otherwise absent themselves from the responsibility of what their organizations do or fail to do.
- A leader remains responsible for decisions and their ultimate success or failure.
- Sports offer the opportunity to observe an individual's true character.
- Individuals should adopt a continuous improvement attitude toward their personal careers.
- Don't take on the king in public. Subordinates should not correct their leaders in open forum. It is not career enhancing.
- Individuals should focus on content, not process.
- In the end, there are two types of people—those who accomplish things and those who talk about those who accomplish things.
- It is important to keep one's morale high.
- Keep it simple. The best plans are those that everyone understands.
- If a request is submitted to an authority on multiple occasions and in different forms, chances are that someone will approve it.
- The busy leader will value the staff officer who can take complicated issues, reduce them to simple terms, and present them in the briefest amount of time.
- Being accessible (to organizational members) will not solve all of a leader's problems, but being inaccessible can be a career terminator.
- Victorious players (leaders) can reach down within themselves and bring to the forefront an inner will that keeps the pressure and the focus on the goal.
- The most successful individuals have sought out the hard jobs.

- If the leader says the same thing twice, it is important. Take note!
- It is the small things that will trap one on the way to the larger goal.
- Maintaining personal contacts at all organizational levels goes a long way in removing barriers to getting the job done.
- In the long run, when one looks back over a career, it is not so much the issues that were won, negotiated, or lost that are important, but the principles by which one lived and worked.
- Never be too busy for your boss.
- An honest and fair compliment about one's contemporary will return handsome dividends.
- People always appreciate the agenda moving faster than expected.
- The subordinate who is both loyal and dependable is very valuable to the organization and will ultimately be rewarded.
- Conduct business as if your actions were going to appear on the front page of the newspaper.
- Can you satisfactorily explain your actions to your mother?
- When you gather 80 percent of the facts—it is time to make a decision.
- Organizations are not bad—but leaders can be.
- Learn to ask the right questions.
- What gets measured gets done.
- There is often 30 percent difference between the original bid and the bottom line.
- Learn to deal successfully with the media.
- The mike is always on.
- Be your employees' cheerleader. Give credit to them.
- Be enthusiastic.

- Think like your boss.
- Never pass up a good opportunity to keep your mouth shut!
- Power corrupts.
- After interpersonal disagreements, make peace quickly.
- Learn to present a "decision briefing" in 15 minutes.
- Know five good things your organization is doing.
- There is no such thing as a "personality conflict" with the boss.
- Never put ugly thoughts in writing.
- Recognize that the difference between success and failure is often only five percent.
- Leaders leave legacies, both good and bad.
- The leader who is willing to share credit and put the organization and its people first will leave a good legacy.
- Remember to accomplish the mission and take care of the employee.

INDEX OF
NAMES AND
PLACES